# How Is Online Pornography Affecting Society?

Christine Wilcox

IN CONTROVERSY

ReferencePoint Press®

San Diego, CA

## About the Author

Christine Wilcox writes fiction and nonfiction for young adults and adults. She has worked as an editor, an instructional designer, and a writing instructor. She lives in Richmond, Virginia, with her husband, David, and her son, Doug.

© 2016 ReferencePoint Press, Inc.
Printed in the United States

**For more information, contact:**
ReferencePoint Press, Inc.
PO Box 27779
San Diego, CA 92198
www.ReferencePointPress.com

Picture credits:
Associated Press: 22
© Jacques M. Chenet/Corbis: 13, 57
© Jason DeCrow/AP/Corbis: 70
Depositphotos: 32
Michael Donne/Science Photo Library: 28
© Cat Gwynn/Corbis: 34
© Andrew Holbrooke/Corbis: 79
Curtis Means/acepixs.com/Newscom: 75
© C. Moore/Corbis: 18
© Julian Stratenschulte/dpa/Corbis: 52
Thinkstock Images: 9, 43, 64
Visual&Written/Newscom: 45

LIBRARY OF CONGRESS CATALOGING-IN-PUBLICATION DATA

Wilcox, Christine.
  How is online pornography affecting society? / by Christine Wilcox.
    pages cm. -- (In controversy)
  Includes bibliographical references and index.
  ISBN 978-1-60152-882-7 (hardback) -- ISBN 1-60152-882-5 (hardback) 1. Internet pornography--Juvenile literature. 2. Pornography--Social aspects--Juvenile literature. I. Title.
  HQ471.W55   2016
  306.77--dc23

                                           2014047679

# Contents

# Foreword

In 2008, as the US economy and economies worldwide were falling into the worst recession since the Great Depression, most Americans had difficulty comprehending the complexity, magnitude, and scope of what was happening. As is often the case with a complex, controversial issue such as this historic global economic recession, looking at the problem as a whole can be overwhelming and often does not lead to understanding. One way to better comprehend such a large issue or event is to break it into smaller parts. The intricacies of global economic recession may be difficult to understand, but one can gain insight by instead beginning with an individual contributing factor, such as the real estate market. When examined through a narrower lens, complex issues become clearer and easier to evaluate.

This is the idea behind ReferencePoint Press's *In Controversy* series. The series examines the complex, controversial issues of the day by breaking them into smaller pieces. Rather than looking at the stem cell research debate as a whole, a title would examine an important aspect of the debate such as *Is Stem Cell Research Necessary?* or *Is Embryonic Stem Cell Research Ethical?* By studying the central issues of the debate individually, researchers gain a more solid and focused understanding of the topic as a whole.

Each book in the series provides a clear, insightful discussion of the issues, integrating facts and a variety of contrasting opinions for a solid, balanced perspective. Personal accounts and direct quotes from academic and professional experts, advocacy groups, politicians, and others enhance the narrative. Sidebars add depth to the discussion by expanding on important ideas and events. For quick reference, a list of key facts concludes every chapter. Source notes, an annotated organizations list, bibliography, and index provide student researchers with additional tools for papers and class discussion.

The *In Controversy* series also challenges students to think critically about issues, to improve their problem-solving skills, and to sharpen their ability to form educated opinions. As President Barack Obama stated in a March 2009 speech, success in the twenty-first century will not be measurable merely by students' ability to "fill in a bubble on a test but whether they possess 21st century skills like problem-solving and critical thinking and entrepreneurship and creativity." Those who possess these skills will have a strong foundation for whatever lies ahead.

No one can know for certain what sort of world awaits today's students. What we can assume, however, is that those who are inquisitive about a wide range of issues; open-minded to divergent views; aware of bias and opinion; and able to reason, reflect, and reconsider will be best prepared for the future. As the international development organization Oxfam notes, "Today's young people will grow up to be the citizens of the future: but what that future holds for them is uncertain. We can be quite confident, however, that they will be faced with decisions about a wide range of issues on which people have differing, contradictory views. If they are to develop as global citizens all young people should have the opportunity to engage with these controversial issues."

*In Controversy* helps today's students better prepare for tomorrow. An understanding of the complex issues that drive our world and the ability to think critically about them are essential components of contributing, competing, and succeeding in the twenty-first century.

# The Internet Is for Porn

T ype the phrase "the Internet is for porn" into Google's search engine and more than 4 million hits will be returned. The phrase is both a joke and a truism—the Internet is responsible for the explosion of modern pornography online. According to neuroscientists Ogi Ogas and Sai Gaddam, authors of *A Billion Wicked Thoughts: What the Internet Tells Us About Sexual Relationships*, "In 1991—before the birth of the Internet as we know it— there were fewer than 90 porn magazines published in the US. Today, more than 2.5 million porn sites are blocked by CYBERsitter."[1] CYBERsitter is Internet filtering software that protects children from inappropriate content. The researchers claim that according to a survey of information collected by popular search engines, approximately 100 million men in North America visit pornography websites per year.

## The Internet Popularized Pornography

Before the Internet, pornography was both risky and expensive to acquire; it was either hidden away in adult sex stores or had to be ordered through the mail. But once pornographic images could be shared over the Internet, they became affordable, accessible, and anonymous—what scholars call the "Triple A Engine" effect. Pornography can now be accessed anonymously at any time on any number of mobile devices—and usually for free. For this reason, both production and consumption of pornography have skyrocketed.

While many of the statistics about the pornography industry are vague and hard to verify, academic researcher Clarissa Smith states that online pornography is now an $8 billion industry in the United States. In 2012 the technology blog *ExtremeTech* estimated that visits to pornography websites account for as much of 30 percent of the Internet's total traffic. "Porn sites cope with astronomical amounts of data," writes senior editor Sebastian Anthony. "The only sites that really come close in terms of raw bandwidth are YouTube or Hulu."[2] According to Anthony, one of the largest online pornography sites has roughly six times the bandwidth of Hulu; it serves more than 100 million page views per day, and during its peak hours it serves four thousand page views per second.

As for how much of the Internet is devoted to porn, most sources cite statistics that claim that one-quarter to one-third of all Internet websites are pornographic in nature. However, more recent studies have shown that these statistics are wildly inflated. "Big numbers are more sensational and make for good press," claims Ogas. "But those big numbers have always been an urban myth."[3] Ogas and Gaddam found that only 4.2 percent of the world's most popular 1 million websites were related to sex. However, they did find that 13 percent of web searches were for pornographic content, which indicates that while pornography may not have taken over the Internet, using online pornography is an extremely popular pastime. It is generally assumed that 70 percent of men and 30 percent of women use online pornography at least occasionally, although those numbers are estimates only, based on a compilation of various surveys.

"In 1991—before the birth of the Internet as we know it—there were fewer than 90 porn magazines published in the US. Today, more than 2.5 million porn sites are blocked by CYBERsitter."[1]

— Neuroscientists Ogi Ogas and Sai Gaddam, authors of *A Billion Wicked Thoughts: What the Internet Tells Us About Sexual Relationships*.

## Difficult to Regulate

Historically, pornography has been difficult to regulate, and once pornography moved online, regulation became virtually impossible. Pornography itself is legal for adults to access—it is considered to be a form of personal expression protected by the First Amendment right to freedom of speech. However, obscenity does not have First Amendment protection. For pornography to be deemed obscene—and therefore illegal—it must both offend moral standards and be devoid of any significant artistic value. Distinguishing between what is obscene and what is merely pornographic is extremely difficult for the courts to do. For this reason, law enforcement now concentrates its efforts on combating online child pornography.

## How Online Pornography Is Used

Although many people enjoy pornographic films as a genre and watch them to be entertained or to learn about different sexual techniques, the primary purpose of pornography is to sexually arouse the viewer. Most people use online pornography during masturbation to enhance their arousal. It is important to understand this because when experts discuss the harms of online pornography use, they usually do not clarify that they are talking about the harms of masturbating to online pornography. For instance, when addiction experts claim that online pornography causes addiction, they are referring to the act of masturbating to climax while viewing pornographic images. Online pornography tends to be much more arousing than traditional forms of pornography, and many theorize that when it is used to aid in masturbation, the extreme and often violent imagery it contains makes a significant impact on the brain.

## The Controversy over Online Pornography

This impact on the brain is why many critics of online pornography claim that it causes sexual dysfunction, reduces desire for real sex, and hijacks the sexuality of young people. It was once also accused of promoting violence toward women, but this has been disproved; the *International Journal of Law and Psychiatry* found that in every country that has studied the issue, as availability of pornography has increased, sex crimes have either decreased or not increased. Anti-pornography activists now focus on educating people about the harms to children and to relationships and the problems associated with addiction. They also warn that addiction to legal online pornography can lead people to seek out illegal pornography, such as child pornography.

Pro-pornography activists claim that harms associated with online pornography are greatly exaggerated, and many believe that

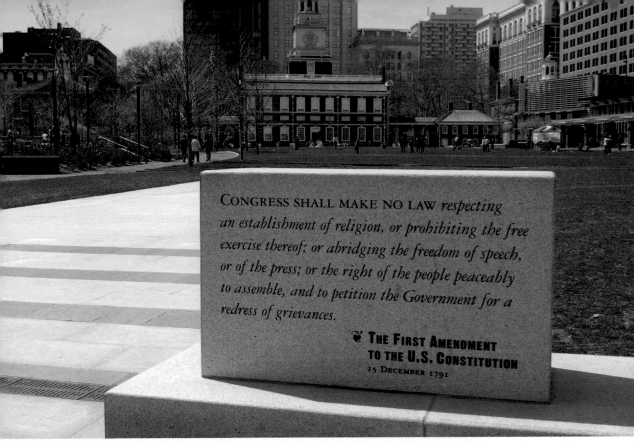

CONGRESS SHALL MAKE NO LAW *respecting an establishment of religion, or prohibiting the free exercise thereof; or abridging the freedom of speech, or of the press; or the right of the people peaceably to assemble, and to petition the Government for a redress of grievances.*

**❦ THE FIRST AMENDMENT TO THE U.S. CONSTITUTION** 15 DECEMBER 1791

pornography addiction is a myth. They point out that the science supporting online pornography's harm is almost nonexistent and that most theories are based on studies of drug and alcohol addiction. These critics believe that current controversies about online pornography are based on a morality that sees masturbation as deviant and supports only sexual expression within loving, monogamous relationships.

## An Individual Choice

Regardless of who is right, online pornography is causing problems for a significant portion of the population. Children are stumbling on inappropriate images and misunderstanding fundamental truths about relationships and sex. Relationships are ending because one partner comes to prefer using online pornography to being intimate with the other. And thousands are using online pornography compulsively and do not know how to stop.

*Pornography, unless it involves minors, is considered to be a form of personal expression. As such, it is protected by the Constitution's First Amendment (pictured here on a stone tablet outside Independence Hall in Philadelphia).*

For these people, help is available—in traditional therapy, 12-step groups, and online support. But in the end, it is up to each individual to decide if online pornography can be a healthy part of sexual expression or if it ultimately undermines happiness and fulfillment.

# CHAPTER ONE

# What Are the Origins of the Online Pornography Controversy?

The history of the controversy over online pornography can be traced back to computer hobbyists in the 1970s and 1980s, who traded pornography on the electronic bulletin board systems (BBSs) that predated the World Wide Web. When personal computers became more affordable in the mid-1990s, a national controversy erupted over how to protect children from accessing online pornography—and perhaps falling prey to sexual predators online. As freedom of speech supporters battled against anti-pornography activists in the courts, the online pornography industry exploded. As it grew, it advanced cutting-edge technologies like e-commerce and streaming media—technologies that are now central features of modern society.

## Before the World Wide Web

Online pornography existed before the World Wide Web, which was not made available to the public until 1993—a date most use to mark the beginning of the modern Internet. Before 1993 the most common way early computer users shared information—including pornographic images—was through electronic BBSs. A BBS is a computer system that allows users to connect to a central computer using a modem (a device that turns digital data into an electrical signal so it can be transmitted over a telephone line or other medium). BBSs became extremely popular with computer hobbyists in the 1980s and early 1990s. Users who dialed in to a BBS through their telephone lines could exchange messages, play simple games, or upload and download text and image files.

Many BBSs contained libraries of pornographic images that had been scanned from magazines or photographs by the BBSs' owners and users, and collecting electronic pornographic images became a popular pastime among computer hobbyists. However, there were plenty of drawbacks to exchanging images in this way. Because bandwidth was limited, it could take an hour or more to download a small black-and-white image, and there was no way to preview the image beforehand. In addition, dialing into a BBS could be costly—long-distance fees charged by the phone company could amount to hundreds of dollars a month.

One of the largest BBSs was Rusty n Edie's BBS. Founded in 1987 by computer hobbyists Russell and Edwina Hardenburgh, Rusty n Edie's was one of the first BBSs to streamline the process of uploading and downloading files. Though the system contained a wide variety of content, it quickly became a popular place to share pornographic images. At its height in the early 1990s, Rusty n Edie's had more than fourteen thousand paying subscribers and boasted forty thousand adult-oriented images available for download.

## The Threat to Children

As computers became more popular among the general public, society became concerned about the amount of pornography being shared over the Internet. In March 1993 the US Department of Justice raided the homes of dozens of American citizens who were downloading child pornography from two BBSs operating in Denmark. Dubbed "Operation Long Arm," the raids were the largest child-pornography operation that had ever been conducted in the United States.

The publicity around the operation brought the issue of online pornography to the attention of the public—many of whom were venturing online for the first time using online services such as CompuServe. That publicity was in part generated by the Justice Department itself, which believed it was important to alert the growing number of computer users to the dangers of pedophiles operating online, especially since children were being encouraged to use computers. The *Los Angeles Times* reported that the head of Operation Long Arm, George Burgasser, "described the computer distribution of pornography as 'more invidious' [more dangerous] than that distributed through more traditional means because it enables 'pedophiles to reach into the homes of at-risk children' through computers and lure them into lewd activities."[4] Thus, online pornography—even if it was adult-oriented and otherwise legal—began to be viewed not just as inappropriate but as intrinsically dangerous to children, making them vulnerable to pedophiles who might use that pornography to bait their victims.

*Computer hobbyists of the 1970s and 1980s used computers like this one to trade pornographic images over electronic bulletin boards. One such bulletin board boasted of having forty-thousand adult-oriented images available for download.*

## The Great Cyberporn Panic

Society's concern about online pornography peaked in what many in the media have dubbed the "great cyberporn panic of 1995."[5] The panic was fueled by a controversial cover story titled "On a Screen Near You: Cyberporn," published by *Time* magazine. The article cited a Carnegie Mellon University study that claimed that 83.5 percent of images on the Internet were pornographic and that trading pornographic images was one of the most common activities taking place over computer networks. The *Time* article sparked fierce debate in the media and on Internet forums, in part because the study—conducted by an undergraduate student and published in a non-peer-reviewed journal— was severely flawed. Vanderbilt University associate professors Donna Hoffman and Thomas Novak claimed that many of the author's statistics were "misleading or meaningless" and "that pornographic files represent less than one-half of one percent of all messages on the Internet."[6] Other Internet experts insisted that most online pornography was locked behind BBS pay walls and difficult for children to access.

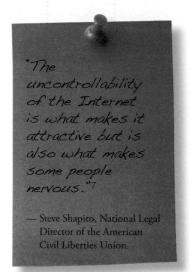

"The uncontrollability of the Internet is what makes it attractive but is also what makes some people nervous."[7]

— Steve Shapiro, National Legal Director of the American Civil Liberties Union.

Despite this, public concern over the issue continued to grow. Steve Shapiro, National Legal Director of the American Civil Liberties Union (ACLU), claimed, "This whole [online pornography] scandal fed into an already existing impulse to control the Internet. . . . The uncontrollability of the Internet is what makes it attractive but is also what makes some people nervous."[7]

## Congress Takes Action

In 1996 Congress passed the Child Pornography Prevention Act (CPPA), which criminalized sharing and receiving child pornography on the Internet. However, the panic over online pornography also spurred an effort to regulate all indecent or obscene material on the Internet. This led to the passage of another law in 1996, the Communications Decency Act (CDA). The CDA was sponsored by democratic senator James Exon and republican senator Slade

Gorton and received bipartisan support in the Senate, passing in an 84–16 vote. It was signed into law by President Bill Clinton on February 8, 1996. The CDA prohibited anyone from sending or making available any obscene or indecent material to children under age eighteen. Violators could be fined up to $250,000 and sentenced to two years in prison for each violation.

The CDA immediately came under intense criticism by the ACLU and other anticensorship advocates, who claimed that restricting speech on the Internet would prevent newspapers from making their content available online, block access to information about issues such as homosexuality and sexually transmitted diseases, and prevent parents from deciding what material was appropriate for their children. A week after its passage, US District Court Judge Ronald Buckwalter blocked enforcement of the CDA until the government defined the term *indecent*. A coalition lead by the ACLU then challenged the law in court, claiming it was too broad and vague to be enforceable and that it violated the First Amendment right to freedom of speech. In an online debate of the issue led by journalist Linda Ellerbee, those who supported the CDA claimed that the Internet should be regulated like television and radio because children had easy access to it. Representative Pat Schroeder claimed that "free speech is for adults" yet "a five-year-old is better at getting on the Internet than I am."[8] Those who were against the indecency provisions of the CDA argued that software was available to parents to prevent children from accessing pornography. ACLU president Nadine Strossen said, "We can't allow the government to stifle it [the Internet] now at the beginning. That would be an enormous tragedy."[9]

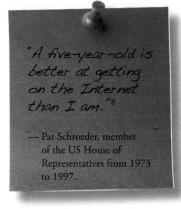

"A five-year-old is better at getting on the Internet than I am."[8]

— Pat Schroeder, member of the US House of Representatives from 1973 to 1997.

On June 26, 1997, the Supreme Court ruled that the anti-indecency provisions of the CDA were unconstitutional. All nine justices agreed that the CDA violated freedom of speech. In the court's opinion, Justice John Paul Stevens quoted from an earlier ruling when he wrote, "As we have explained, the Government may not 'reduce the adult population . . . to . . . only what is fit for children. . . . Regardless of the strength of the government's

## Constitutional Challenge to the CDA

In 2005 the National Coalition for Sexual Freedom challenged the constitutionality of the obscenity provision of the CDA. The legal challenge was made on behalf of Barbara Nitke, a fine arts photographer who displays photographs depicting alternative sexuality on her website. According to the CDA, obscenity is determined by local community standards. In the lawsuit, Nitke argued that she and other artists like her risk prosecution for obscenity at any time because they have no way to know which areas in the United States might consider their work to be obscene. Nitke said, "It's impossible to know who's going to find what obscene, so everybody just has to make a guess at where the lines are." She argued that, because fears of prosecution caused artists to censor their own work, the law had a chilling effect on free speech and was therefore unconstitutional.

A federal district court in New York ruled against Nitke, claiming that she did not present enough evidence about varying community standards to make her case. Nitke appealed to the Supreme Court, which affirmed the lower court's decision without comment.

Quoted in Randy Kennedy, "An Online Artist Challenges Obscenity Law," *New York Times*, July 28, 2005. www.nytimes.com.

interest' in protecting children, 'the level of discourse reaching a mailbox simply cannot be limited to that which would be suitable for a sandbox.'"[10] Other provisions of the CDA, including the ban on obscenity, remained in effect.

## Protect the Children

After the indecency provisions of the CDA were overturned, the government concentrated its efforts on shielding children from pornography. In 1998 Congress passed the Child Online Protection Act. The act forced all commercial Internet sites that distributed material considered by contemporary community standards to be harmful to minors to prevent minors from accessing their sites. The law was immediately blocked by the courts because the law would apply to any depiction of nudity, sexual acts, or anything else that provoked sexual thoughts. After a series of court battles, it was overturned in 2007.

Portions of the Child Pornography Prevention Act of 1996 were also challenged in the courts. The act criminalized virtual child pornography—which included any pornography that appears to be performed by a minor (such as adults dressed as children). It also criminalized any image that conveys the impression that a minor is engaging in sex (such as when it is implied that an underage actor has had sex off-screen). The Free Speech Coalition challenged the law in 2002, claiming that the law would criminalize famous works of art such as Shakespeare's *Romeo and Juliet*. In *Ashcroft v. Free Speech Coalition*, the Supreme Court struck down these provisions of the act. In the court's decision, Justice Anthony Kennedy wrote, "The statute prohibits the visual depiction of an idea—that of teenagers engaging in sexual activity—that is a fact of modern society and has been a theme in art and literature throughout the ages."[11]

*"The level of discourse reaching a mailbox simply cannot be limited to that which would be suitable for a sandbox."[10]*

— Supreme Court justice John Paul Stevens on why the indecency provision in the Communications Decency Act is unconstitutional.

In 2003 the PROTECT Act (which stands for Prosecutorial Remedies and Other Tools to end the Exploitation of Children Today) included the reinstatement of the ban on virtual child pornography. This includes computer-generated images that are indistinguishable from pornography involving actual children (for instance, images that have been altered with software like Photoshop). Although the ban was again challenged, it was eventually upheld by the Supreme Court in 2008. The ban also includes the possession of art or illustrations depicting child pornography (such as cartoons depicting children having sex) because the images can be used by pedophiles to entice children to perform sexual acts (a process known as "grooming"). Currently, these representations of child pornography are legal in many other countries and therefore can be easily found online.

*The sunny San Fernando Valley in Los Angeles (pictured) is the hub of the US pornographic film industry. The Internet and advances in digital technology have helped the industry grow.*

## Online Pornography's Golden Age

Despite the legal battles over Internet censorship and pornography, the period from 1997 to 2006 saw enormous growth in the online pornography industry. After the anti-indecency provisions of the CDA were overturned in 1997, the US pornographic film industry, which is based in California's San Fernando Valley, began to explore offering its products online. The Internet offered distinct advantages to its customers, such as privacy and relative anonymity. Also, the new digital technology behind DVDs (introduced in 1997) also allowed for digital downloads, which would let people view pornography in the privacy of their own homes without having to rent or purchase it at a video store or have it delivered through the mail. This created a huge demand for digitalized pornographic films. By 2002 "everyone [in the pornography industry] was making money," explained Michael Stabile, a journalist who writes about pornography. "Internet startups had started to figure out streaming video, and you could still sell DVDs all day long. Hundreds of new companies sprouted, like mushrooms after a rainstorm. . . . It was the beginning of porn's golden age."[12]

Streaming media technology (first developed by a Dutch pornography company called Red Light District in 1994) led to the development of webcam technology, which was used for private pornographic web chats online. By 2003 Apple and Microsoft were designing and selling webcams commercially. All of this created a need for more bandwidth and faster download speeds. According to "Ten Indispensible Technologies Built by the Pornography Industry," an article by technology blogger Paul Rudo, "Demand for sexual content drove the market for improved routers, switches, relays and other fundamental Internet infrastructure. Early users consistently sought faster, easier and more reliable connections through which to trade increasingly bandwidth-hogging pornographic text, photographs and video."[13]

## E-commerce

Despite the sudden demand for online pornography, in the late 1990s e-commerce was still in its infancy, and online transactions were looked on with suspicion by the general public. In addition, the dot-com boom of 1997–2000 was in full swing. Most Internet companies were concerned about growing as large as possible and then cashing in by selling shares on the stock market, not in developing new revenue streams such as e-commerce.

The pornography industry was the first business sector to partner with new online credit card transaction companies that were developing safe and secure e-commerce practices. The 2009 film *Middle Men* is about the most successful of these e-commerce entrepreneurs, Christopher Mallick. "We got a percentage of each [DVD] sale," Mallick explains. "At the height of the business, we were doing about $1.3 billion a year in credit card billing."[14] These early efforts in online commerce demonstrated to other industries that consumers were willing to make credit card purchases online. And as the pornography industry grew, it continued to be on the forefront of innovation in online commerce. As attorney Frederick Lane, author of *Obscene Profits: The Entrepreneurs of Pornography in the Cyber Age*, explains:

> The porn industry has served as a model for a variety of online sales mechanisms, including monthly site fees, the provision of extensive free material as a lure to site visitors, and the concept of upselling (selling related services to people once they have joined a site). In myriad ways, large and small, the porn industry has blazed a commercial path that other industries are hastening to follow.[15]

## The Obscenity Prosecution Task Force

As the demand for online pornography grew, there was also a demand for more extreme sexual images and activities. For instance, because of the 2002 ruling in *Ashcroft v. Free Speech Coalition* (which lifted the ban on pornography that implied that sex was occurring between minors), pornography featuring youthful-looking actresses dressed as young teens became legal. This genre of pornography became known as "barely legal" porn and was extremely successful. Another genre that was gaining popularity was gonzo porn. Gonzo began as a style of pornographic filmmaking that put the viewer in middle of the scene—it is often shot with handheld cameras by the actors and features graphic close ups. Gonzo porn also does away with story and focuses on the sexual act, usually in graphic detail, and is considered by most to be hardcore porn. It is the predominant style of pornography that exists on the Internet today.

In reaction to the explosion of hardcore pornography available online, in 2005 social conservatives urged the George W. Bush administration and the Justice Department to create the Obscenity Prosecution Task Force. Obscenity is illegal in the United States, but because it is hard to prove, it is rarely prosecuted. The definition of *obscenity* is determined by a three-part test established by the 1973 ruling in the court case known as *Miller v. California*. According to the Miller test, local community standards must find that the material in question appeals to prurient, or sexual, interests; portrays sexual activity as defined by a locality's obscenity law; and lacks serious artistic, political, or scientific value. Conservatives believed that much of the pornography online was obscene and that its creators and distributors should be prosecuted.

## The Great Recession of 2008–2009

The online porn industry reached its height in 2007. According to the Internet filtering company Covenant Eyes, Internet porn was a $3 billion-a-year industry in 2007, and by 2008 more than forty thousand websites distributed pornography. Then on September 15, 2008, a major financial panic broke out in the United States, and stock markets crashed all over the world. Economies stayed in recession until June 2009, and the pornography industry was particularly hard hit.

*Police in China confiscate pirated pornographic DVDs. Pirating has cut into profits of the global pornography industry.*

To survive the economic downturn, many pornography companies consolidated. "Companies who have consolidated have a definite advantage," explains pornographic studio head Chris Ward. "There are efficiencies in scale that smaller companies can't match."[16] Ward merged his company with the video-on-demand giant, ADEN (Adult Entertainment Broadcast Network), and he now heads the largest production company in the gay pornography industry.

The industry also suffered from Internet pirating—the illegal viewing and sharing of copyrighted material online. Much of this pirated material began showing up on tube sites, which became extremely popular in the wake of the recession. Tube sites are platforms from which individuals can upload content for others to stream for free. (YouTube is the most popular non-pornographic tube site.) Because videos on tube sites can be viewed on demand for free (the site earns ad revenue from page views, but the copyright holders earn nothing), tube sites cut deeply into the revenue of the pornography industry's traditional distribution methods. The Free Speech Coalition estimated that the global pornography market has lost at least 50 percent of its revenue since 2007 due to pirating and tube sites. The most popular tube sites are owned by MindGeek, a huge pornography company based in Luxembourg that now monopolizes the industry. According to the website On the Media, MindGeek operates nearly one hundred pornographic websites, has more than 100 million visitors daily, and uses more bandwidth than Facebook, Twitter, or Amazon.

Today, almost all pornographic film studios that have not adapted to the online marketplace have disappeared. The companies that remain are exploring new ways to market their products online that will draw consumers away from tube sites. Some companies are distributing pornography on mobile devices such as tablets and phones—platforms that are difficult to pirate. Others are eliminating monthly subscriptions and adapting a micropayment structure made popular by online retailers like iTunes. These micropayment systems allow users to pay a small amount for each video after setting up an account.

## A Social Controversy

The downturn of the pornography industry has also caused filmmakers to produce content that is more graphic and hardcore. Anti-pornography activists like Gail Dines believe that the demand for more graphic content is caused by the tendency for people to become desensitized emotionally after repeated exposure to extreme images. Dines believes the extreme gonzo porn available online today is responsible for pornography addiction and violence against women. She also contends that the desensitization process is driving more and more people to seek out illegal pornography such as child pornography. She also believes that extreme porn is damaging to young people and should be regulated. "Free porn is the equivalent of me standing outside a high school handing out free cigarettes and alcohol," she claims. "This would not be allowed, so why is the porn industry the one industry that should not be regulated?"[17] Other activists believe the extreme nature of today's online pornography causes pornography addiction, which they claim causes a host of problems, including sexual dysfunction.

Despite current concerns about pornography addiction and pornography's effect on young people, the US government currently has no plans to regulate the industry. Even though obscenity is still illegal, most efforts by law enforcement have focused on fighting child pornography, not adult obscenity. This was made apparent in 2011, when the Obscenity Prosecution Task Force was essentially shuttered by Attorney General Eric Holder, who folded it into the Child Exploitation and Obscenity Section of the Justice Department. Controversy over online pornography has moved into the social realm, where activists work to educate the public about the dangers to children, to relationships, and to those prone to addiction.

## Facts

- The first example of computer art was an illustration of a pin-up girl, displayed on the screen of a $238 million military computer in the late 1950s.

- Like BBSs, Usenet operated on the Internet before the World Wide Web was opened to the public. Usenet newsgroups were popular places to discuss and trade online pornography, including child pornography.

- A 1994 Carnegie Mellon University study of early pornography on computer BBSs found that 48 percent of downloads were for deviant or illegal sexual acts, while less than 5 percent depicted traditional intercourse.

- According to the Internet security software company Websense, the number of websites that were dedicated to pornography went from eighty-eight thousand in 2000 to nearly 1.6 million in 2004.

- In 2001 a Forrester Research report found that the average age of a male visitor to pornography websites was forty-one and his annual income was $60,000.

- A Google Trends analysis indicates that searches for teen porn, also known as "barely legal porn," have more than tripled between 2005 and 2013. In March 2013 searches for teen porn represented one-third of total daily searches for pornographic websites.

# CHAPTER TWO

# How Addictive Is Online Pornography?

**W**hen activists speak of online pornography addiction, they often describe it as a health crisis. Donna Rice Hughes, chief executive officer of the anti–online pornography organization Enough Is Enough, says, "The Internet pornography pandemic has become one of the greatest global threats to children, marriages, families and nations. No one is immune."[18] However, in the medical community, there is a great deal of controversy over whether pornography addiction exists. Until recently it was thought that only chemical substances could cause addiction. However, in the 2013 revision of the *Diagnostic and Statistical Manual of Mental Disorders* (*DSM-5*)—the manual that mental health professionals use to diagnose illnesses—a single behavioral addiction was added: gambling disorder. Proponents of the theory of pornography addiction claim that if gambling can be addictive, then sexual activities such as using pornography must be as well. As addiction expert Stanton Peele asserts, "Is gambling really more neurologically, or intensely, rewarding than sex?"[19] In fact, many pornography addiction experts say that online pornography causes such a powerful reaction in the brain that it can actually cause addiction in individuals who are not prone to addiction.

"The Internet pornography pandemic has become one of the greatest global threats to children, marriages, families and nations."[18]

— Donna Rice Hughes, chief executive officer of the anti–online pornography organization Enough Is Enough.

26

# What Is Addiction?

In order to understand the debate over whether pornography is addictive, one first must understand what addiction is. Even though the term *addiction* is frequently used to describe the over-consumption of everything from chocolate to Facebook, *addiction* is a medical term with a specific definition. According to the American Society of Addiction Medicine, "Addiction is a primary, chronic disease of brain reward, motivation, memory and related circuitry."[20] For a substance to be classified as addictive by the US Food and Drug Administration, it must contain powerful chemicals that change the structure of the brain in significant ways. As the National Institute on Drug Abuse explains, "Brain-imaging studies from people addicted to drugs show physical changes in areas of the brain that are critical for judgment, decisionmaking, learning, memory, and behavior control."[21] In other words, addictive substances physically rewire the reward pathways in the brain, which in turn changes behavior. Addiction is something physical that happens to a person's brain, regardless of his or her mental strength or willpower.

Once the brain has adapted to the presence of an addictive substance, it becomes physically dependent on it. Sudden removal of the substance will cause a painful readjustment period known as withdrawal. Withdrawal, which can be physical or psychological, is one of the defining characteristics of addiction. Psychological withdrawal occurs when a person has developed an emotional dependence on a substance and experiences emotional distress in its absence. Physical withdrawal occurs when the body has adjusted to the effects of the substance and must readjust to its absence. Physical withdrawal can be painful and even dangerous; the withdrawal symptoms of alcohol addiction can sometimes cause fatal convulsions. Some substances are so addictive that they always cause physical dependence and withdrawal, regardless of whether or not an individual is psychologically dependent on the drug. For instance, people who become addicted to morphine after a long hospitalization must have their dose gradually reduced or they will suffer painful withdrawal symptoms such as body cramps and vomiting—regardless of whether or not they crave the drug.

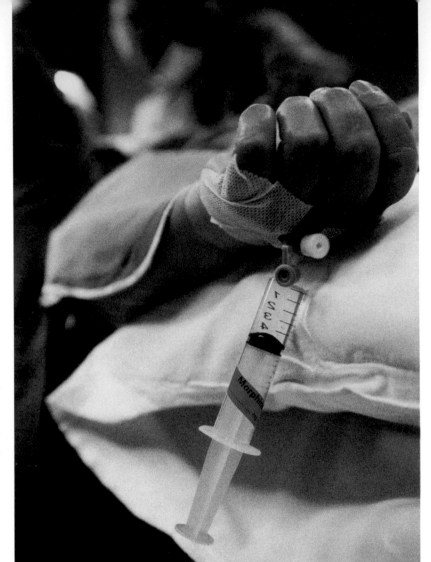

*A patient receives morphine during surgery. Prolonged use of morphine during a long hospital stay can lead to addiction and a painful withdrawal process. Some experts believe that online pornography is similarly addictive and difficult to stop using.*

## Behavioral Addictions

Also known as process addictions, behavioral addictions are a new class of addiction included in the *DSM-5*. However, only one behavioral addiction was included: gambling addiction. Pornography addiction was not included, because not enough research has been done on its effects on the brain.

Behavioral addictions are patterns of behavior that follow a cycle similar to substance addictions. According to psychologist and addictions expert Elizabeth Hartney, "When the person is addicted, they experience urges or cravings to engage in the behavior, which intensify until the person carries out the behavior again, usually feeling relief and elation. Negative consequences of the behavior may occur, but the individual persists with the behavior in spite of this."[22] Like substance addictions, behavioral addictions include aspects of tolerance to the effects of the behavior, increased use, and withdrawal symptoms if the behavior is stopped. Other behavioral addictions include Internet addiction, shopping addiction, and sex addiction.

## What Is Pornography Addiction?

Pornography addiction is a type of sex addiction. However, whereas sex addicts almost always have a history of abuse or mental health issues, pornography addicts usually do not. Pornography addiction experts believe that modern online pornography is powerful enough on its own to cause addiction—even if an individual is not otherwise vulnerable to addiction.

People who are addicted to online pornography spend an excessive amount of time using pornography despite negative consequences. They become desensitized over time to milder forms of pornography and seek out more explicit and intense forms—a process that some experts claim corresponds with the tolerance substance abusers experience. Once addicted, online pornography addicts find it difficult to stop the behavior. If they do stop, the withdrawal symptoms they experience tend to be milder than those experienced by substance abusers, and the symptoms tend to be psychological rather than physical. Reported withdrawal symptoms include headaches, anxiety, anger, sweating, depression, insomnia, loss of energy, hypersensitivity, chills, and heart palpitations. Most people report an inability to stop thinking about the addictive behavior, which can trigger intense and uncomfortable cravings.

## The Process of Pornography Addiction

Pornography addiction experts claim that using online pornography can cause a cascade of powerful chemicals to be released in the brain. For instance, the sensation of sexual desire is caused by the release of testosterone in both men and women. The novelty

## The Pornography Industry
## May Encourage Addiction

The pornography industry's current business model may be encouraging—or even causing—pornography addiction. According to journalist and anti-pornography activist Martin Daubney, the largest pornography company, Manwin (now known as MindGeek), tracks specific details about the types of pornography each user clicks on and the duration of time that they spend watching it. Using a complex algorithm, Manwin's website then offers each user a menu of pornographic videos that is progressively more explicit and extreme. "By continually offering racier porn, so begins the path towards converting you into a paying customer," Daubney writes. "'Personalized porn' is the future: free porn as a gateway to paid, real-life webcam or escort services, HD quality porn, and stuff too racy even for mainstream broadcast." The industry estimates that approximately 10 percent of pornography users will ultimately pay to access specialized content.

Martin Daubney, "Porn Users Don't Realize They Are Being Watched," *Telegraph* (London), February 5, 2014. www.telegraph.co.uk.

and surprise associated with online pornography causes the release of dopamine, which is associated with craving and want. Norepinephrine is one of the chemicals released during orgasm, causing exhilaration and enhancing the individual's memory of the experience. Oxytocin is also released, flooding the body with pleasurable sensations. According to the website of one pornography addiction treatment program, "During porn viewing, the brain releases a tidal wave of endorphins and other powerful neurochemicals like dopamine, norepinephrine and serotonin. These natural 'drugs' produce a tremendous rush or high. All over the world people are using pornography as a drug-of-choice."[23]

One reason that online pornography is so powerful is that the online medium lets a person view a wide variety of sexual images in a single sitting. Variety and surprise are tied to physical arousal—at least in males. One Australian study found that men who watched the same erotic scene eighteen times in a row were less and less aroused on each viewing. But when they were showed a different scene the nineteenth time, their arousal increased dramatically. This response is activated by online pornography because the medium encourages users to click from scene to scene, rewarding the viewer with surprising and shocking images, each of which release dopamine in the brain.

Many experts think that because variety and surprise are inherent in online pornography, it can be more arousing than sex with a partner. The brain is tricked into believing that it has repeated opportunities to mate and rewards each new image with a burst of dopamine. "Each novel female on a guy's screen is perceived as a genetic opportunity,"[24] explains Gary Wilson, founder of the website Your Brain on Porn. "Internet pornography offers endless fireworks at the click of a mouse. You can hunt (another dopamine-releasing activity) for hours, and experience more novel sex partners every ten minutes than your hunter-gatherer ancestors experienced in a lifetime."[25] These surges of dopamine quickly overload the brain's chemical receptors, which absorb the circulating dopamine and translate it into feelings of want, pleasure, and satisfaction.

"Internet pornography offers endless fireworks at the click of a mouse."[25]

— Gary Wilson, science writer and founder of the website Your Brain on Porn.

## Tolerance and Escalation

The brain responds to the flood of extra dopamine by reducing some of its dopamine receptors. This protects the overloaded brain by limiting the amount of dopamine that can be absorbed. Once this happens, the amount of pleasure the brain experiences is reduced as well. The brain then needs more extreme forms of porn to achieve the same "high," or initial level of pleasure or arousal.

According to Fight the New Drug, it is not a weakness of character or a vulnerability to addiction that causes a person to want to repeat the high caused by online pornography. Instead, it

*A succession of pornographic images can be easily viewed with the click of a mouse. Each image stimulates production of dopamine in the brain, heightening feelings of want, pleasure, and satisfaction.*

is the extremely stimulating nature of online pornography itself. Organizations like Fight the New Drug believe that with repeated use, the cycle of tolerance and escalation will ultimately lead to addiction in almost anyone—especially if they start using online pornography at a young age, when the brain is still developing. As psychiatrist Jeffrey Satinover explained to a US Senate committee, "It is as though we have devised a form of heroin . . . usable in the privacy of one's own home and injected directly to the brain through the eyes."[26]

Even though organizations like Fight the New Drug believe that constant exposure to pornography causes the same kind of tolerance and escalation that drug users experience, some researchers disagree. Instead, they believe what is actually happening is simply a process of desensitization. Humans tend to become desensitized to any graphic or disturbing image or scenario over time. For instance, emergency room clinicians are known for being desensitized to signs of physical trauma. Pornography users may also become desensitized to some types of images and scenarios, but that does not mean they will experience the intense craving and inability to stop that afflicts drug addicts. "There are no sex receptors in the brain to develop tolerance and dependence, as there are with alcohol and drug addiction,"[27] explains Dr. Eli Coleman, who directs the program in human sexuality at the University of Minnesota Medical School. He suggests that sexual addictions like pornography addiction are more likely to be a psychological problem related to impulse control or compulsive drive rather than true addiction.

## Escalation and Gonzo Pornography

Whether or not desensitization to online pornography is equivalent to tolerance to an addictive drug, the process of escalation is what causes pornography addicts the most harm. Escalation is the process of feeling the need to seek out more and more explicit, taboo, and violent pornography. Anti-porn activist Gail Dines spends part of every lecture showing scenes from gonzo pornography to her audiences to illustrate what today's porn users are seeking out, and many are shocked by what they see. "A lot of women who call themselves feminists don't know what's in porn,"[28] says Dines, noting that these women believe today's porn is similar to what was once depicted in *Penthouse* magazine. Dines also believes that women who claim that they enjoy pornography are not watching gonzo. "[Gonzo is] the sort of thing you used to have to go to the back of an adult store to find," she says. "Now, it's mainstream. . . . The sex is always aggressive and often presented as non-consensual, with girls crying and screaming."[29]

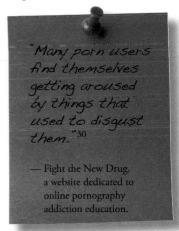

"Many porn users find themselves getting aroused by things that used to disgust them."[30]

— Fight the New Drug, a website dedicated to online pornography addiction education.

Watching gonzo pornography can cause viewers to feel ashamed that they are aroused by violent, denigrating images. According to Fight the New Drug, "Many porn users find themselves getting aroused by things that used to disgust them or that go against what they think is morally right."[30] Still, many of them will seek these images out and even pay a premium for videos that are progressively more shocking and taboo because they are unable to get aroused in

*The workplace has become a common venue for looking at online pornography. One business site claims that one-fourth of employees who use the Internet admit to watching porn during work hours.*

any other way. According to Dines, the makers of gonzo porn exploit this fact. She says that pornographers are always trying to find "some new, edgy sex act that will draw in users [who are] always on the lookout for that extra bit of sexual charge."[31]

## When Porn Takes Over

The consequences of watching gonzo pornography go beyond feelings of guilt and shame. Experts say that online pornography can consume a person's life, isolating them from normal social interactions. "Porn became the center of my days," says Neil, a twenty-nine-year-old accountant in Galway, Ireland. "I would start thinking about porn the minute I woke up in the morning. If a friend called over to my house in the evening and stayed a while, I'd get really irritated."[32] Little by little, Neil began withdrawing from his friends until he found himself leaving his own birthday party to go watch porn. "The funny thing is, I never thought porn was the problem," he says. "I blamed other things for taking up my time—my work, phone calls from friends and family, even doing my washing! It wasn't until my birthday that I knew something was very wrong with me."[33]

Neil feels lucky that he stopped before the urge to watch porn spilled over into the workplace, but others are not so lucky. Watching online pornography at work has become surprisingly common. "A full one-quarter of employees who use the Internet admit to watching porn during work hours," reports AllBusiness.com. "It's a statistic backed up by the porn industry, which reports that 70 percent of its traffic is generated during business hours."[34] Being caught watching porn at work can have devastating consequences, ruining professional reputations and careers.

## Leads to Using Child Pornography Online

The most concerning effect of online pornography desensitization, escalation, and addiction is that addicts who have become desensitized to legal porn sometimes move on to illegal porn, such as child pornography. Many who seek out these images are not pedophiles; they are not aroused by the children they see on a day-to-day basis and have no urge to have sexual contact with a child. Instead, they are aroused by the shame and taboo that surrounds child pornography. Addicts who have been caught up in the escalation process have been arrested, jailed, and branded sexual predators for life because child pornography has been found on their computers.

Some experts believe that online child pornography can actually create a pedophile—especially if the viewer is already a porn addict. Dines interviewed a number of men who were serving sentences for raping children. All had used online child pornography, but not because they were attracted to children—at least initially.

"What they said to me was they got bored with 'regular' porn and wanted something fresh," Dines explained. "They were horrified at the idea of sex with a prepubescent child initially but within six months they had all raped a child."[35] If these criminals are to be believed, then the process of desensitization and escalation can extend into the real world, turning a pornography addict into a sex offender or even a pedophile.

## Harmful, but Not Addictive

Even though it is clear that habitual use of online pornography can cause great harm, many addiction specialists argue that behavioral addictions like online pornography are not true addictions. They claim that behaviors like eating, having sex, or viewing pornography release just a fraction of the dopamine that powerful drugs like heroin and cocaine release, and therefore the physical process of tolerance and withdrawal cannot occur. They note that very few studies have ever been done on the effects of pornography on the brain, and the few that have are inconclusive. For instance, in 2013 a study published in *Socioaffective Neuroscience and Psychology* exposed fifty-two pornography addicts to sexual images while examining their brain waves. The study's authors expected to find that the addicts' brains would mimic the responses of drug addicts. Instead, they found no correlation between the intensity of the individuals' level of addiction and their brain's responses to pornography. Only their overall level of libido, or sexual desire, corresponded to how intensely their brain waves responded to sexual imagery.

To date, only two studies have shown that pornography addiction is similar to drug addiction. In 2014 neuropsychiatrist Valerie Voon used brain imaging to measure the brain response of self-described sex addicts to pornography. She found that when the addicts looked at pornographic images, the pleasure centers of their brains "lit up" with the same intensity as that seen in drug addicts. A second study in Germany got similar results. However, critics claim that the two studies do not prove addiction because addiction is a physical process that is not defined by brain activity at a single point in time but by changes in the brain. In response to

## Christians Report High Levels of Pornography Addiction

A survey cited in a Christian handbook titled *A Parents' Primer on Internet Pornography* states, "50 percent of Christian men and 20 percent of Christian women are addicted to pornography." While no verification is given for these statistics, other surveys have confirmed that the incidence of self-reported pornography addiction tends to be higher among Christians. This may be because Christians are encouraged to see any pornography use as sinful and may be more likely to believe they are addicted. "As an expression of brokenness, pornography takes God's good gift of sexuality and twists it all around," the handbook states. It goes on to claim that pornography causes people to believe that "people are sexual objects to be used for our own pleasure" and "to dominate someone sexually is more fun and enjoyable than mutual sexual pleasure between a married husband and wife."

Some pro-pornography advocates believe that pornography addiction experts also view pornography through a moral lens. These addiction experts claim that to recover from pornography addiction, a person must engage only in positive sexual encounters with a spouse or primary partner—a position similar to the Christian view of healthy sexuality.

Walt Mueller, *A Parents' Primer on Internet Pornography,* CPYU's Digital Kids Initiative, Center for Parent/Youth Understanding, 2014. www.digitalkidsinitiative.com.

Voon's findings, sex therapist Marty Klein writes, "That's the same part of the brain that lights up when we see a sunset, the Golden Gate Bridge, the perfect donut, a gorgeous touchdown pass, or our grandchild's smile. Our brain, our blood, and our hormones always react to pleasure—including sexual pleasure."[36]

## Bad Science

Another criticism of the theory of pornography addiction is that it is based on bad science. Psychologist David Ley notes that a recent review of the current scientific literature on online pornography addiction found that less than 1 percent of it was reliable or useful to other scientists. "The literature is weighted with moral and cultural values. There are tons and tons of theoretical statements that are made but never evaluated," he says. "Less than one in four actually have data. In less than one in 10 is that data analyzed or organized in a scientifically valid way."[37]

One problem Ley sees in the research is that most of it presents correlation (A and B are both observed) as causation (A causes B). For instance, research has found that many people who frequently use pornography are also depressed. It is scientifically invalid to take this correlation—depression and pornography use—and assume that pornography causes depression. However, most of the literature on pornography addiction assumes just that. Ley notes that it is just as likely that depression leads to increased pornography use. "Sexuality and sexual arousal is a very effective, perhaps the most effective, method of distracting oneself from negative emotions,"[38] he says.

Another problem Ley sees is that pornography addiction specialists tend to blame pornography addiction for their clients' problems rather than looking at why the person is using pornography. "There is consistent evidence that higher levels of libido and higher levels of sensation-seeking and higher levels of sexual sensation-seeking seem to predict higher levels of porn use,"[39] he explains. But instead of evaluating the whole person, pornography addiction treatment providers tend to focus only on quitting pornography. This does not address why the person had the need to watch pornography in the first place, Ley says, which means that the issues that caused that need are likely to continue to negatively affect the person's life.

## A Growing Problem

Whether or not online pornography is addictive, studies show that there are a significant number of people who are having problems controlling their online pornography use. One survey of more than nine thousand Internet users who were not predisposed to addiction found that 7.5 percent believed they had become addicted to pornography. A 2014 survey conducted by the Barna Research Group found that among American men, 44 percent think they may be watching too much porn, and 18 percent—or 21 million men—believe they may be addicted to porn. The numbers are lower for women, but they are still significant. Nineteen percent think they may be watching too much porn, and 3 percent—or 3 million women—think they may be addicted. And although fewer women use pornography overall, studies have shown that women who view online pornography become addicted at the same rates as men. A 2011 study published in *Cyberpsychology, Behavior, and Social Networking* found that the rate of pornography addiction among German women who regularly viewed pornography was about the same as it was among men.

## More Research Is Needed

It is still unclear whether pornography is addictive and capable of causing a behavioral addiction—in part because very few studies have been done. It is also unclear whether there is anything inherently addictive about pornography that is transmitted over the Internet, which tends to be extremely explicit and highly arousing, and which gives users the ability to click through a variety of images and scenes in a short period of time. The issue is not likely to be resolved until research into pornography addiction is adequately funded.

"Sexuality and sexual arousal is a very effective, perhaps the most effective, method of distracting oneself from negative emotions."[38]

— Psychologist David Ley, author of *The Myth of Sex Addiction.*

# Facts

- In 2009 University of Montreal researcher Simon Louis Lajeunesse made headlines when he announced that he could not proceed with his study on online pornography because he could not find a man in his twenties who had not seen pornography.

- According to Richard Land, president of Southern Evangelical Seminary, among eighteen- to thirty-year-old Christian men, 36 percent view pornography daily and 32 percent claim they have an addiction.

- According to the website Stop Porn Culture, in the United States two-thirds of human resource workers have found pornography on employees' work computers.

- According to an infographic published by Online Schools, 20 percent of men and 13 percent of women admit to watching online pornography at work.

- According to one of the web's largest porn sites, American's porn-watching sessions are, on average, the longest in the world. Americans spend an average of 10 minutes and 39 seconds on the website every time they visited.

# CHAPTER THREE

# Is Online Pornography Harmful to Young People?

The controversy over online pornography and its effects on children is about relative harm. Anti-pornography activists claim that online pornography warps the sexual development of young people and can lead to addiction. As sex and intimacy expert Alex Allman claims, "There is a coming tsunami of sexual dysfunction from the younger generation that is going to ruin relationships, break hearts, crush marriages, and leave confused unhappiness where there might have been epic love."[40] Pornography defenders say that warnings like Allman's greatly exaggerate the risks to young people and play on parents' fears. They also point out that there is no reliable scientific data that proves that online pornography is harmful to youth—or to anyone.

## Parents Misinformed

In the United States the job of controlling what children see online generally falls to parents. However, according to anti-pornography activists, adults who do not watch online pornography often do not realize how extreme and violent it has become. Many remember their own experiences with pornography, which are often limited to *Penthouse* magazine or films on the Playboy Channel that would be considered tame by today's standards. These adults tend to dismiss concerns over young people watching pornography, and many neglect discussing pornography with their kids altogether.

A review of readers' comments to the *New York Times* article "So How Do We Talk About This: When Children See Online Pornography" confirms this. About half of the commenters thought concern over children accessing pornography was overblown. One commenter wrote, "In my pre-Internet childhood, I searched for pornography and found it. . . . I was never traumatized, and seeing it as early as age six did not destroy my teen or adult love-life."[41] Another wrote, "Is there damage to a child occasionally seeing sexually explicit material on the Internet? Of course not. . . . Sex, remember, is actually healthy, and good for you."[42] A third said, "I'd be more worried about the teenage boy who does NOT look at pornography on a regular basis."[43] Interestingly, when a commenter tried to point out how "extremely violent" most online pornography had become, the post was blocked by the online moderator. "My comment, which simply listed some common pornographic scenarios, appears to have been moderated out," the commenter wrote. "This confirms that typical pornography has gone beyond the realm of 'natural' sexual activity."[44]

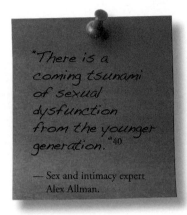

"There is a coming tsunami of sexual dysfunction from the younger generation."[40]

— Sex and intimacy expert Alex Allman.

## Stumbling on Pornography

Even though today's youth are exposed to a highly sexualized media environment, many are unprepared for what they see online. The average age for a child to see online pornography is eleven years old—though most experts believe that many children stumble upon online porn much earlier. This happened to one six-year-old girl from upstate New York, who accidentally clicked on a link to a pornographic video while watching *My Little Pony*. The results can be traumatic. Another girl, age twelve, saw sex for the first time on the Internet at a friend's house. It was a typical scene in contemporary online pornography—three people having rough sex. She was horrified. "[After] I came home, I was bawling my eyes out," she admitted. "I'll never forget it."[45]

Gail Dines says that once teen girls get over their shock, they tend to be angry and frustrated that so much pornography shows females enjoying disrespectful and often brutal behavior. Dines believes that boys are equally traumatized if pornography is their first introduction to sex. She describes the experience of a typical eleven- or twelve-year-old boy curious about pornography:

> When he puts porn into Google, what does he think is going to come up? Probably pictures of breasts, maybe a naked woman. In reality . . . he is catapulted into a world of sexual violence, sexual cruelty, [and] body punishing sex. He does not have a reservoir of his own experiences of sexuality with other people—he's probably never had sex with another human being. This is his first introduction to sex. . . . I would go so far as to argue that [this experience] is sexually traumatizing an entire generation of boys."[46]

*Young Internet users can easily stumble upon pornographic images while online. The experience can be traumatic for some of these kids.*

## Advanced Knowledge

Many children start watching porn not because they are seeking it out, but because sharing online material has become part of social interaction. "I try not to look at it, but people just keep sending it to each other," said one fifteen-year-old boy. "They email disgusting links to each other's mobile phones to shock."[47] This practice has created a generation of children who are extremely knowledgeable about deviant sexuality. For instance, Johnny Hunt, a sex education specialist who is known for his frank discussions of sexuality, regularly encounters kids who know about sexual practices or fetishes that he has never heard of. Hunt starts his sessions by asking kids to make an A–Z list all of the sexual terms that they know. Anti-porn activist Martin Daubney filmed one of Hunt's sessions with a class of thirteen- to fourteen-year-olds in the United Kingdom for his documentary, *Porn on the Brain.* "The children's extensive knowledge of porn terms was not only startling, it superseded that of every adult in the room—including the sex education consultant himself,"[48] Daubney writes. He also notes that every child in the class had seen sodomy acted out in porn videos, and many of the children he interviewed had seen pornography that depicted illegal acts.

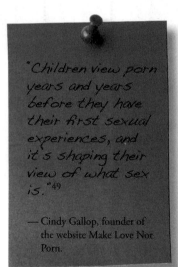

"Children view porn years and years before they have their first sexual experiences, and it's shaping their view of what sex is."[49]

— Cindy Gallop, founder of the website Make Love Not Porn.

According to Cindy Gallop, a former advertising executive and the creator of several sex-positive websites, the problem is not that young people have an inappropriate level of sexual knowledge; the problem is that they are using pornography to learn about sex. "Children view porn years and years before they have their first sexual experiences, and it's shaping their view of what sex is,"[49] Gallop says. Psychologist Rory Reid, who researches the effects of pornography on young people, agrees. "I have a son," he says, "and I don't want him getting his information about human sexuality from Internet porn because the vast majority of such material contains fraudulent messages about sex—that all women have insatiable sexual appetites, for example."[50]

The county of Warwickshire in England decided to address the issue head on. County officials created a website called Respect

Yourself designed to educate children about sexuality and dispel the myths about sex that online pornography perpetuates. According to the website, "Because pornography is something we don't talk about openly, except to say how awful and damaging it is—we leave many confused young people feeling isolated and unable to ask for help."[51] Kids are encouraged to submit questions to the site and read the questions and answers submitted by others. Unfortunately, the website uses frank language about sexuality and is blocked by most Internet filtering software.

## Teens Understand the Problem

Even teens realize that pornography influences their understanding of real sex. Forensic psychologist Miranda Horvath organized a group of sixteen- to eighteen-year-olds to debate whether or not pornography had an impact on them. The pro-impact group had a lot of insight into the issue. "They said it had an impact on their body image, on what young people think sex should be like, what they could expect from sex," Horvath said. "They talked about how if you see things in pornography, you might think it's something you should be doing and go and do it."[52] The no-impact group did not have much to contribute and could not fill their fifteen minutes of debate time.

Researchers have found that girls are especially aware of how pornography shapes sexual expectations, and many of them are angry about how it impacts what boys expect of them. Daubney, who noticed this when he filmed Hunt's sex education class, writes:

> One 15-year-old girl said, "Boys expect porn sex in real life." And one boy—to choruses of approval—spoke of his revulsion for pubic hair, which he called a "gorilla." When Johnny [Hunt] pointed out that pubic hair was normal in real life, the boys scoffed, but some of the girls were angry that the boys' template of what to expect from real girls had clearly already been set by porn.[53]

Dines has observed the same thing in her interviews with young people. "When you interview young women about their experiences of sex, you see an increased level of violence: rough, violent sex," she says. "That is directly because of porn, as young boys are getting their sexual cues from men in porn who are acting as if they're sexual psychopaths."[54]

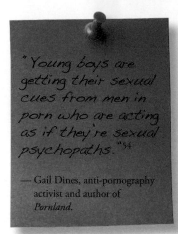

"Young boys are getting their sexual cues from men in porn who are acting as if they're sexual psychopaths."[34]

— Gail Dines, anti-pornography activist and author of *Pornland*.

## Preferring Porn to Sex

Robert Weiss, an expert on the treatment of online pornography addiction, believes that the disconnect between what children learn about sex through pornography and what sex is really like can lead to some young adults preferring pornography to real-world sex. He notes that many experts believe that children's "brains are being rewired to demand unrealistic levels of novelty, stimulation, and excitement, and, as a result, they are becoming totally out of sync with real-world romantic relationships."[55] As these children become young adults, they sometimes decide that sex is less arousing and less physically satisfying than porn. Two large-scale surveys in Japan

## Teens Understand That Porn Is Not Realistic

Anti-pornography activists have expressed concern that online pornography misinforms teenaged boys about what constitutes typical sexual behavior. A Swedish study published in the *Journal of Sex Research* that surveyed seventy-three teens aged fourteen to twenty indicates that this may not be true. Although the girls in the study were concerned that boys who watched pornography would want to act out the sexual behavior they saw in porn, the boys in the study denied this. Study authors Lindroth Löfgren-Mårtenson and Sven-Axel Månsson write, "[The boys] asserted that sex in real life is something completely different from sex in porn." The authors said that the boys insisted they could tell the difference between porn sex and real sex in the same way that they could differentiate between cartoon violence and real violence. Both boys and girls in the study claimed that they understood that online pornography was not realistic.

Quoted in Michael Castleman, "How Does Internet Porn Affect Teens—Really?," *Psychology Today*, May 17, 2011. http://www.psychologytoday.com.

confirm that this is happening. In a 2008 survey 17.5 percent of males aged sixteen to nineteen said they were either uninterested or averse to having sex with another person. Two years later, the percentage had doubled to 36.1 percent. While the study does not link porn use to a lack of interest in sex, Weiss suggests that increased porn use may be the cause. "This rising disinterest in real-world physical intimacy coincides directly with the online porn explosion, which began in earnest right around 2008," he writes. "So it appears the new reality for at least some young men is that, thanks to online porn, they are less motivated than their predecessors to seek traditional forms of in-the-flesh sexuality."[56]

# Hijacked Sexuality

Gary Wilson believes that the reason some young men come to prefer using pornography to having real-life sexual encounters is because they have developed a brain-based sexual dysfunction. According to Wilson, visitors to his site recount stories of using porn since they were twelve or thirteen years old and then, during their first sexual encounter at seventeen, being unable to become aroused. Wilson explains that those early years of using online pornography "have trained their brain to need to sit and watch and be a voyeur and need a certain level of stimulation in order to get sexually excited."[57] Also, because children's brains are still forming and are malleable, they tend to respond more intensely to emotionally charged material. Since pornography is emotionally charged—especially when it is combined with the sexual arousal of a teenager—rituals and habits that accompany pornography use may become ingrained in a young person's neural pathways. Some experts believe that if the association between porn use and arousal continues until adulthood, the adult may find that he or she cannot become aroused in any other way. In a sense pornography has hijacked their sexuality.

Journalist Isaac Abel has concluded that Wilson's theory explains what happened to his own sexuality. Abel believes that the difficulties he had with sex as a young man are directly related to his pornography use as a child. In elementary school he and his friends would burn CDs of the pornography they found on the Internet and swap them back and forth. In middle school sneaking on the family computer to watch porn late at night became an obsession. He began to seek out more graphic and hardcore images until he felt ashamed of the content he was drawn to. During his senior year, he decided to quit using pornography altogether, but it seemed that the damage had been done—he found that he had difficulty having intercourse. Once he found a steady girlfriend, he discovered he needed to fantasize about pornography to have intercourse. "It was a dissociative, alienating, almost inhuman task to close my eyes while having sex with someone I really cared about and . . . recall a deviant video from the archives of my youth that I was ashamed of even then."[58] Even now, Abel finds that his sexual fantasies are rooted in the pornography he watched at fourteen—images that he chose simply because they were extreme and deviant, not because he had an innate interest in them.

## Teens Are More Vulnerable to Addiction

Experts on pornography addiction also believe that teens are even more susceptible to pornography addiction than adults. This is because parts of the teenaged brain have not yet matured. The prefrontal cortex—the part of the brain responsible for willpower and self-control—does not fully develop until about age twenty-five. However, the reward centers are fully developed—pleasure and reward chemicals fire in a teenager's brain with the same intensity as in adults. This is why teenagers tend to impulsively seek out pleasurable activities, even though they know they are harmful. Daubney writes, "The brains of teenagers are not wired to say 'stop,' they are wired to want more."[59]

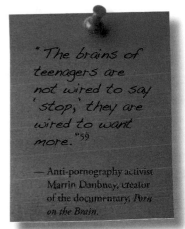

"The brains of teenagers are not wired to say 'stop,' they are wired to want more."[59]

— Anti-pornography activist Martin Daubney, creator of the documentary, *Porn on the Brain*.

Because many teens lack the ability to moderate their actions, they often find themselves repeating addictive activities in excess. Many experts believe this speeds up the process of addiction. And once they are addicted, teens face the same consequences that adults do. For instance, teens addicted to porn often use it as a go-to coping mechanism for the stresses of life. This can cause problems, especially when young people move from high school to college or work and have to deal with more stress and less privacy. Other consequences can be especially hard on teenagers because they tend to be more concerned about being "normal" and are less emotionally equipped to deal with toxic feelings like shame. This can lead to isolation and stunted social development that can continue far into adulthood.

## Teen Sexting Is Child Pornography

The same lack of self-control that causes teens to seek out more and more graphic pornography can also result in them becoming involved in sexting. Sexting is exchanging nude or sexually

## Porn Can Hijack Sexuality in Girls

Young women are not immune to the hijacking effects of pornography. While fewer girls watch pornography than boys, those who do seem to be just as susceptible to its influence on their sexuality. Violet, who read Isaac Abel's article "Did Porn Warp Me Forever?," told Abel she has problems similar to his due to her use of online pornography as a young teenager. She never felt as though she was addicted to porn, but she believes that watching it profoundly affected her developing sexuality. Violet identifies as a lesbian, but because she watched straight pornography when she was younger, she has a hard time aligning her fantasies with her sexual orientation. "I've been brainwashed so that anytime I experience erotic feelings they channel through mainstream hetero porn images." She describes this as "the involuntary internal hijacking of erotic expression."

Quoted in Isaac Abel, "Was I Actually 'Addicted' to Internet Pornography?," *Atlantic*, June 7, 2013. www.theatlantic.com.

provocative pictures on a mobile device. Most of the controversy over sexting has to do with girls being pressured by boys to send nude pictures of themselves, which are then circulated or posted online. However, young people who sext often do not realize that nude pictures of minors (anyone under eighteen) are considered by federal law to be child pornography. A conviction for distributing child pornography carries a mandatory minimum sentence of five years in prison. Thus, a seventeen-year-old girl who texts a nude picture of herself to her boyfriend is technically distributing online child pornography—as is her boyfriend, if he forwards it to anyone else.

The consequences of sexting can be dire. In May 2014 eight teenagers faced online child pornography charges after posting nude pictures of local high school teens on Instagram, a photo-sharing social networking site. According to KTUU-TV in Anchorage, Alaska, police interviewed more than fifty students and seized more than one thousand images from twenty electronic devices. The charges filed against the eight juveniles ranged from possession to distribution. "A lot of these images were 'selfies.' They were taken by the individuals themselves,"[60] said Detective James Estes. He explained to the *Washington Post* that if a teenage boy took a picture of his genitalia and sent it to his girlfriend, the boy could be charged with manufacturing and distributing child pornography and the girl could be charged with possession.

## Sexting, Bullying, and Suicide

A few states have passed laws that decriminalize sexting to protect impulsive teens from being charged with multiple felonies, but Alaska has not. Neither has New Jersey, where Allyson Pereira experienced years of bullying and being ostracized at her high school after texting a topless picture of herself to her boyfriend—who then distributed it to his entire contact list. Even after her family home was repeatedly vandalized, Pereira feared asking the police for help because she had been told that she could face charges of manufacturing and distributing child pornography online. She now speaks out in favor of decriminalizing sexting among minors. "All it takes is for you to press 'send' and in a millisecond it's out there and you can't take it back," she says. "[Girls] just impulsively send it. They don't think of the consequences. And the same with the boys who are passing it on. They don't think about how it might affect the person who's pictured."[61]

Pereira believes that the bullying made her a stronger person, but many girls have a different experience. Reports of teenagers committing suicide after their nude images are posted online have become common in the news. The website CyberBully Hotline reports that 42 percent of teenagers endure at least one incident of cyberbullying, and 10 percent of those bullied attempt suicide. While it is unknown how many of these incidences are related to sexting, a 2013 survey conducted by MTV found that 30 percent of teens report being involved in naked sexting. Of those,

17 percent admit to forwarding sexts to other people. Essentially, teens whose sexts are forwarded or posted have become the subjects of online pornography against their will.

## No Proof of Harm

Despite the wealth of anecdotal evidence about the dangers online pornography poses to teens, no scientific studies exist that actually prove harm. Such studies would be difficult to do because it is illegal to expose minors to pornography. Researchers also have a hard time securing funding for studies because of concerns about ethics. "A lot of [funding] review boards see this kind of research as a ticking time bomb," says Reid. "Universities don't want their name on the front page of a newspaper for an unethical study exposing minors to porn."[62]

Instead, online pornography experts must apply what they know about how young brains react to sexual trauma, violent video games, or addictive substances to online pornography—essentially making an educated guess about its effects. This has been a major criticism by those who do not believe that online pornography is harmful or that pornography addiction exists. According to psychologist David Ley, author of *The Myth of Sex Addiction*, "In good addiction research, what we find is that there is a transition from a person wanting to use a substance to needing to use a substance, and we can see that transition in their brain. There is absolutely no scientific evidence to date that there is such a transition related to pornography."[63]

Scientists who have reviewed existing studies of children and pornography reached a similar conclusion. They found that no scientific studies prove for certain that pornography causes any type of harm to children. In the United Kingdom the office of the Children's Commissioner for England studied 276 research papers on teenagers and pornography. They were trying to find some proof that viewing pornography increased risky behavior in young people, but they concluded that there was no evidence that pornography in any way caused risky or harmful behavior. A group of American researchers performed a similar review and reached the same conclusion. According to Eric Owens, an assistant professor at West Chester University and a coauthor of the review study, "By the end we looked at 40 to 50 studies. And it became, 'O.K., this one tells us A, this one tells us B.' To some degree we threw up our hands and said, there is no conclusion to be drawn here."[64]

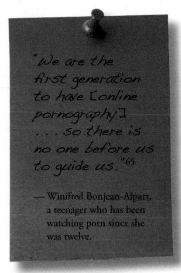

"We are the first generation to have [online pornography] . . . so there is no one before us to guide us."[65]

— Winifred Bonjean-Alpart, a teenager who has been watching porn since she was twelve.

## Young People Need Guidance

The debate over online pornography's effects on young people continues. What is clear, however, is that unlike previous generations, today's youth have easy access to extremely explicit and violent sexual imagery. Unless their parents educate them about what they see, society offers no context or guidance about how to handle these emotionally charged images. As Winnifred Bonjean-Alpart, a teenager who has been watching porn since she was twelve, tells ABC Nightline, "We are the first generation to have what we have, so there is no one before us to . . . guide us. We are the pioneers."[65]

# Facts

- Neuroscientists Ogi Ogas and Sai Gaddam have found that the sexual interests that men form in adolescence —when most first encounter pornography—rarely change over the course of their lives. In contrast, women's sexual interests change frequently throughout their lives.

- In a Canadian study of students aged thirteen to fourteen, 90 percent of males and 70 percent of females admitted to accessing porn at least once.

- A poll of five hundred British teenagers found that 80 percent felt it was too easy to accidentally view explicit images while surfing the Internet.

- According to a 2012 survey by TRU Research, 32 percent of teens admit to accessing online pornography. Of these, 43 percent do so on a weekly basis.

- According to a 2014 report of online activity by Covenant Eyes, 15 percent of boys and 9 percent of girls have seen child pornography, 32 percent of boys and 18 percent of girls have seen bestiality, and 39 percent of boys and 18 percent of girls have seen sexual bondage.

- According to the *Journal of Adolescent Health*, prolonged exposure to pornography leads to a belief that promiscuity is normal and that marriage is sexually confining.

# CHAPTER FOUR

# How Does Online Pornography Affect Relationships?

The use of pornography by people in relationships is not new. Some use it in secret, whereas others use it with the knowledge (and often with the participation) of their romantic partners. Opinions about the role of pornography in relationships tend to fall into two camps. One side views pornography as a subversive force in a relationship, debasing and trivializing the loving bond between two people. The other side sees pornography as a harmless pastime or even a tool—a way for a couple to spice up their sex life by watching together for mutual enjoyment or inspiration.

The advent of online pornography and growing concerns about addiction have given rise to the idea that pornography is destructive to relationships. Dozens of anti-pornography groups and hundreds of individuals are speaking out about pornography on the Internet, claiming that it destroys a person's desire to be intimate with a partner, causes erectile dysfunction, and ultimately kills love and ends relationships. These claims are not confirmed by scientific evidence. But they are supported by countless stories of online pornography destroying otherwise loving relationships.

## Online Pornography Versus Traditional Pornography

According to online pornography experts, the reason that so many people suddenly have a problem with pornography in their relationships is the same reason that online pornography addiction is on the rise. Compared to traditional pornography, online porn is easy to get and easy to hide, and it offers endless variety. Before online pornography, porn collections were made up of physical objects (such as magazines, VHS tapes, and DVDs) that took up space and usually needed to be hidden from family members. VCRs and DVD players tended to be kept in a common area in the home and could not be used privately. New material was expensive to buy, and renting from the local video store was difficult to do anonymously. In short, it was hard for a person in a relationship to keep porn use secret. For these reasons, most people tended to stop—or at least cut down on—their pornography use after they began cohabitating with a partner.

Online pornography changed all of that. It solves the problems of space and privacy and offers variety at little or no cost. Online porn can be used discretely on a home computer, a laptop, or a mobile device, and today's users can experience an endless variety of scenes without having to flip through a magazine or change a DVD. In short, because of the anonymity and convenience of online pornography, relationships are no longer a barrier to pornography use.

## Online Pornography Separates Couples

Even though online pornography is easy to hide, a suspicious partner with some computer knowledge can usually find evidence of pornography use on a computer or mobile device. When this happens, feelings of hurt and betrayal are common. However, because online pornography can be extremely explicit and violent, many partners also feel confusion and shock—especially if the offended partner has never seen gonzo-style pornography.

Psychologist Kevin Skinner believes that the discovery that a partner is watching online porn can actually cause emotional

trauma. Skinner surveyed more than four thousand people who were seeking help with online pornography use for themselves or for their partners. (In the majority of cases, the men were the ones seeking help for themselves and the women were seeking help for their partners.) Eighty percent of the women reported that, since the discovery, they felt anxious at least half of the time, 84 percent felt emotionally on edge, and 75 percent felt fear. "My research indicates that many women are experiencing trauma," Skinner writes in *Psychology Today.* "These real-life challenges make relationship bonding and connection much more difficult."[66]

Even when one partner knows about the other's online porn use, it can still cause problems in a relationship. Pornography addiction specialist Tony Lister explains that this is because online pornography is designed to provide much more intensity than the average sexual encounter between long-term partners. "It's like a drug," he explains. "You can't compete with it."[67] Eventually, the porn-using partner begins to prefer the excitement of online

*Secretive viewing of pornography was more difficult when it was only available in magazines and videos or DVDs. Online porn is much easier to access without anyone else knowing about it.*

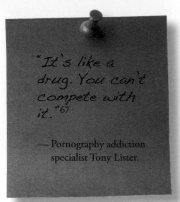

pornography to real-life sexual encounters with his or her partner. Lister describes a common scenario in which a wife has given a husband permission to watch online pornography: "The guy will become less interested in his wife, from a purely biological standpoint, and will become more interested in the intensity pornography offers. That creates a rift [in the relationship], and the wife begins to feel used. . . . And when a woman feels used she is not going to want to have sex anymore."[68]

Lister explains that when a wife gives permission to her husband to use online pornography, she does not expect to then have to compete with the computer screen for attention. If the result of this conflict is less intimacy in the relationship, the husband often feels justified in his pornography use, which causes an even deeper rift. The cycle continues, Lister says, until the relationship is destroyed.

## Online Pornography Can Cause Low Self-Esteem

Some experts have found that people who know about their partners' pornography use also tend to have feelings of low self-esteem. A 2012 study of 308 women published in the journal *Sex Roles* found a link between online pornography use and relationship problems. According to researchers Destin Stewart and Dawn Szymanski, female partners who thought their partners' online pornography use was problematic had more problems with self-esteem and reported poorer relationship quality and lower sexual satisfaction. The women's most common complaint was feeling that they were not as attractive as the female performers online. According to Robert Weiss, the study showed that "it is clear that the repeated use of porn by men in otherwise committed relationships can and often does adversely affect partners."[69] Even women who like online pornography confirm this. Journalist Vicki Larson writes, "I happen to like porn, but a lot of women get tweaked by porn in part because they think their partner is comparing them to Jenna Jameson and other porn stars; we can be competitive—or insecure—when it comes to other attractive women."[70]

Not all women feel threatened by the women in online pornography. While many anti-pornography activists claim that porn portrays images of women that are idealized, some women see online pornography as a place that celebrates diversity. A survey of sixty women by the Canadian magazine *VICE* found that most felt more accepting of their female body parts because they saw so much variety in the sizes and shapes of those body parts in female porn stars. Overall, the women surveyed found online pornography to be a positive tool rather than a source of anxiety.

## Not Just a Male Problem

Although it is more common for women to report feelings of dissatisfaction about their male partner's porn use, women who watch online pornography are just as likely to become addicted and eventually prefer it over their partner. This happened to Maria, who tells her story on the anti-pornography website Fight the New Drug. When Maria discovered that her boyfriend used online pornography, it did not bother her—in fact, she started to watch it with him and found she enjoyed it, too. However, after they got married, they both got into the habit of watching alone. Eventually, they stopped being intimate with each other altogether, which Maria blames on the addictive nature of online pornography. "I had no idea that we had this poisonous ingredient in our relationship, spoiling us from the inside out," she says. "When you realize that you both would rather look at a computer screen and you don't even want to be with each other, it's just really sad." Maria realized too late that when online pornography replaces sex, it removes the opportunity for intimacy and emotional bonding that sex provides a couple. "I've always enjoyed the intimate part of a relationship," she says. "When that went away—it blindsided me. Oh, it was heartbreaking."[71]

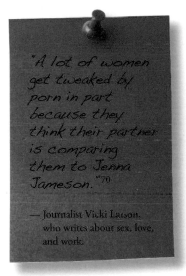

"A lot of women get tweaked by porn in part because they think their partner is comparing them to Jenna Jameson."[70]

— Journalist Vicki Larson, who writes about sex, love, and work.

## Online Pornography Kills Desire for Real Sex

According to Gary Wilson, one reason why people begin to prefer online pornography to sex with their partners is that dopamine can

## Women See Female Pornography Actors as Real People

Experts believe that one reason women can become insecure about their partners' use of online porn is that they tend to see female porn actors as real people rather than as fantasy sex objects. Even women who have watched porn in the past can still feel threatened when constantly exposed to their partner's online pornography. For instance, an online commenter to a poll in *Essence* magazine wrote that she and her husband used pornography as foreplay, but once her husband discovered online pornography, he started using it by himself, turning it into a hobby. After the commenter was diagnosed with breast cancer, her husband continued to display his pornography collection on his computer screensaver in their bedroom. "I had a constant reminder (pictures) of women with healthy breasts while I recovered," she explains. "To my husband, it is not a big deal—I stopped trying to explain how his [collection] made me feel." The commenter's husband considered the porn stars in his collection to be fantasies and did not understand why she felt threatened. However, she identified them as real women—women who could arouse her husband with assets that she did not have—in this case, healthy breasts.

Jasmine, commenter to Sylvia Obell, "*Essence* Poll: Does Porn Warp Your Real-Life Expectations of Sex?," *Essence*, May 27, 2014. www.essence.com.

change the triggers that cause arousal. When the constant variety and surprise in online pornography floods the brain with dopamine, the brain begins to rewire itself. This process of rewiring is called neuroplasticity—the ability of the brain to create new neural pathways and connections that can make it easier for an individual to repeat a behavior. In other words, a habit is formed. A habit is an activity that is cued with triggers instead of with conscious thought. When using online pornography becomes a habit, it can become associated with triggers such as boredom, being home alone, anxiety, stress, or even simply sitting down at a computer.

And arousal becomes linked to cues associated with pornography rather than those associated with courtship. "Behaviors that are associated with [online pornography] are being alone, voyeurism, clicking, searching, multiple tabs, fast forwarding, constant novelty, shock and surprise," Wilson says. "In contrast, real sex is courtship, touching, being touched, smells, pheromones, emotional connection, and interaction with a real person."[72] This is why many people who are addicted to online pornography (or who are on their way to becoming addicted) find that they are no longer aroused by their partners. Dopamine has changed their sexual triggers.

## Erectile Dysfunction

The rewiring of sexual triggers is thought to contribute to a phenomenon called pornography-induced erectile dysfunction. Erectile dysfunction, or ED, is a condition in which a man has difficulty getting or sustaining an erection or having an orgasm. While there is no scientific proof that online pornography causes ED, there is plenty of anecdotal evidence. A survey of twenty-eight thousand Italian men found that long-term exposure to online pornography caused users to eventually lose their ability to get an erection with a partner. According to the study's lead researcher, psychologist Carlos Forsta, the problem begins with a decrease in the ability to become aroused by pornography. "Then there is a general drop in libido and in the end it becomes impossible to get an erection."[73]

The survey confirms the stories that hundreds of men have shared on the Internet about their struggles with online pornography and ED. Many complain that even when they feel attraction for their spouses, they no longer can become physically aroused. Arousal can occur only during online pornography use, but as ED progresses, some find even that difficult. Men who are not in relationships who develop addiction and ED find that it contributes to their lack of motivation—as well as their lack of self-esteem—when it comes to approaching women for relationships.

Many men find that once they quit using online porn, their ED—as well as a host of other symptoms associated with addiction—disappear. For instance, this twenty-eight-year-old quit using online porn after fourteen years of use and reports:

> I've been approached by quite a few women, but they quickly flew away due to my incredible weirdness. I've been a hardcore porn addict since the age of 14. I finally realized porn has been an issue. I stopped it completely 2 months ago, it has been very difficult but so far incredibly worthwhile. My anxiety is nonexistent. My memory and focus are sharper than they've ever been. I feel like a huge chick magnet, and my ED is gone too. I seriously think I had a rebirth, a second chance at life.[74]

## Experts Disagree

Psychologist David Ley does not believe that online pornography can cause ED. "It is more likely that men who are masturbating more frequently, and masturbating more frequently to pornography, are more likely to be in a refractory period where their body has difficulty becoming aroused when they try and have sex," he explains. A refractory period is the period of time after an orgasm when a male cannot physically have an additional orgasm. "One thing we see is the more people masturbate, the longer their refractory periods,"[75] Ley says. He believes that constant masturbation extends the refractory period so that it interferes with normal arousal. According to Ley, that means the issue is not that online pornography has special properties that make it addictive; the issue is that excessive masturbation can make sexual arousal more and more difficult.

Ley also worries that the pornography activists are applying scientific concepts of addiction to online pornography in order to promote their message that the only healthy way to express sexuality is through a loving primary relationship. "There is an assumption in the porn addiction field that using porn and masturbation is negative and unhealthy in some way," he

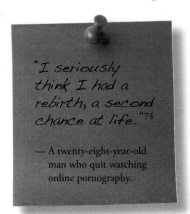

"I seriously think I had a rebirth, a second chance at life."[74]

— A twenty-eight-year-old man who quit watching online pornography.

writes, "but that is a critically unevaluated assumption that is very heavily driven by cultural bias and norms."[76]

Ley thinks that online pornography use is a symptom, not a cause, of relationship problems, and that most of them stem from partners having mismatched levels of sexual drive. "There is consistent evidence that higher levels of libido and higher levels of sensation-seeking . . . seem to predict higher levels of porn use,"[77] he explains. Sex and gender politics author Nichi Hodgson agrees. She writes, "I'm probably in possession of a higher sex drive—and the energy reserves to power it—than many of my male peers. But once in a relationship, I'm enthusiastically monogamous. Without porn, there'd definitely be a sexual energy deficit I'd have to discharge somewhere else."[78] According to Hodgson, online pornography gives a partner with a higher sex drive a way to meet his or her needs without going outside the relationship.

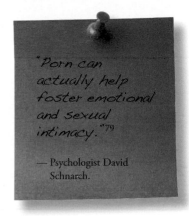

"Porn can actually help foster emotional and sexual intimacy."[79]

— Psychologist David Schnarch.

## Help for Relationships

Therapists who deal with sexuality and relationship issues have long suggested that couples use pornography to enhance their relationships. There is a great deal of evidence that pornography can be useful and therapeutic, fostering closeness and communication between couples. The School of Family Life at Brigham Young University recently hosted a study of more than six hundred committed couples that examined the way that pornography affected their sexual desire and sexual and relationship satisfaction. The study found that when pornography was viewed alone, it impacted negatively on relationships and sexual satisfaction. However, when viewed together, watching pornography increased both partners' sexual satisfaction.

According to psychologist David Schnarch, "Porn can actually help foster emotional and sexual intimacy." Schnarch and his wife run a couples therapy practice in Colorado. "A significant portion of our work in helping couples develop a deeper sexual connection . . . through erotic images,"[79] he explains. He claims that pornography helps couples develop shared fantasies and can inspire them to experiment more and ultimately engage in a more varied and satisfying sexual life.

*Some couples use pornography to enhance their sexual intimacy. Therapists say pornography can be a useful tool when both partners in a relationship watch together.*

Hodgson agrees. She views pornography as a wonderful addition —but a poor substitute—to a healthy sexual relationship. "Porn isn't a substitute for skin-on-skin experience. It's an enhancement, an aperitif," she writes. "It can also provide fantastic inspiration."[80]

## Divorce and Infidelity

One claim that anti-pornography activists often make is that online pornography is responsible for an increase in divorce. Patrick F. Fagan, director of the Center for Research on Marriage and Religion, claims that pornography is a "quiet family killer."[81] He says that pornography not only contributes to infidelity, but pornography use is a factor in more than half of divorces. Fagan bases this claim on data provided by the American Academy of Matrimonial Lawyers. In 2003 it polled 350 attorneys and found that 56 percent of their divorce cases involved issues relating to the compulsive use of online pornography. According to organization president Richard Barry, "Pornography had an almost nonexistent role in divorce just seven or eight years ago."[82]

However, current data about divorce rates does not indicate that online pornography is responsible for an increase in divorces. In fact, as online pornography became more popular, the overall divorce rate has decreased. For instance, a 2011 report from the US Census Bureau shows the rate of divorce in 1996 for women aged forty to forty-nine (the most common decade of life for divorce) was 40.5 percent. In 2009 that rate dropped to 35.6 percent. The United Kingdom has observed a similar drop in divorce rates. According to the British newspaper the *Guardian*, in 2002 the divorce rate in England and Wales was 13.3 per thousand people. In 2012 the divorce rate dropped to 10.8 per thousand—a 19 percent decrease. Although there is no doubt that online pornography can negatively affect relationships, according to these statistics it does not appear that the rise in popularity of online pornography corresponds with an increase in the rate of divorce.

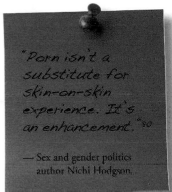

"Porn isn't a substitute for skin-on-skin experience. It's an enhancement."[80]

— Sex and gender politics author Nichi Hodgson.

Though online pornography use probably does not result in more divorces, it may result in more instances of infidelity—especially since many people consider watching pornography in secret itself a form of infidelity. "If you approach infidelity as a continuum of betrayal rather than an either/or proposition, then the Internet era has ratcheted the experience of pornography much closer to adultery than I suspect most porn users would like to admit,"[83] writes Ross Douthat in the *Atlantic* article "Is Pornography Adultery?" Infidelity is a leading cause of divorce, but couples will often seek help for online pornography addiction before they end their relationship. What often happens instead, says sex therapist Marty Klein, is that once illicit pornography use

## Some Men in Relationships Use Addiction as an Excuse

Some experts claim that the reason there seems to be an epidemic of pornography addiction is that people in relationships are using it to explain why they secretly watch pornography. Sex therapist Marty Klein claims that he sees this all the time in his practice. He says that when women catch their partners watching pornography, they sometimes prefer to believe that addiction is to blame because a medical problem is easier to forgive than selfish behavior. "If a wife claims that porn use is infidelity, if a girlfriend claims that porn use means he isn't attracted to her, a disease [like addiction] is a good place to hide," Klein says. In Klein's experience, both men and women embrace this option because it makes it easier to save the relationship.

Marty Klein, "Porn Addict or Selfish Bastard? Life Is More Complicated than That," *Sexual Intelligence* (blog), *Psychology Today,* May 6, 2011. www.psychologytoday.com.

is discovered, the spouse using it will promise to stop. Klein says that although some do stop, "the rest will do what they did when they were 14—they'll do it in secret, feel bad about it and hope they won't get caught. And so a life of lying about sex continues. You can imagine what that will do to the couple's closeness."[84]

## Communication Is the Key

It is still unclear whether online pornography is causing problems in relationships that are otherwise healthy. Couples who report having problems because one partner is using too much online pornography may have reported similar problems if online pornography did not exist. These include problems such as infidelity, mismatched sexual drive, or an addiction to traditional pornography. But some anecdotal evidence suggests that it is the addictive nature of online pornography itself that is to blame, not any underlying problems in relationships. Regardless of whether online pornography is a symptom or a cause of relationship problems, experts encourage couples to have frank discussion about online pornography before it becomes an issue.

## Facts

- According to neuroscientists Ogi Ogas and Sai Gaddam, women are less likely to pay for pornography online. Only about 2 percent of all subscriptions to pornography sites are paid for by women.

- According to a study published in *Social Science Quarterly*, Internet users who have had an extramarital affair were 3.18 times more likely to have used online pornography than those who had remained faithful to their partners.

- A study published in *Sexual Addiction and Compulsivity* found that among the 68 percent of couples in which one person was addicted to Internet porn, one or both had lost interest in sex.

- According to a survey of members of NoFap, a social media community on Reddit, 60 percent of members reported an improvement in their ED as a result of abstaining from masturbation and viewing online pornography.

- A 2012 University of Florida study of 308 heterosexual women aged nineteen to twenty-nine found that the more a woman's partner watched pornography, the less satisfied she was with the relationship.

# CHAPTER FIVE

# What Should Be Done About Online Pornography?

**A**s people debate whether online pornography poses a legitimate risk to society, they also must contend with the issue of what, if anything, can be done about it. The US Constitution protects all forms of speech—including legal pornography. For this reason, using the law to regulate online pornography has had mixed results. Many activists have turned to other methods; some work to educate people about the dangers of online pornography, while others help individuals overcome its effects. Still others believe that online pornography is harmless and attempting to regulate it is a form of censorship. These anti-censorship activists fight to overturn existing laws and prevent new ones from being passed.

## Obscenity Laws

In the United States most federal laws attempting to regulate online pornography have been overturned by the court system—usually because the laws violated the constitutional right to freedom of speech or placed an undue burden on businesses. However, these laws do not address what most anti-pornography activists claim is the real problem: the graphic and violent nature of hardcore online pornography.

The reason that lawmakers are not addressing this issue is that it is already illegal to produce or distribute obscene materials in the United States. Groups like Morality in Media want the obscenity laws enforced. "It is a violation of federal law to distribute obscene [hardcore] pornography on the Internet—and it's all over the Internet," Morality in Media chief executive officer Patrick Trueman told CNS News. Trueman would like to see the Justice Department prosecute the largest producers and distributors. "A handful of these distributors are controlling most of your commercial pornography websites on the Internet," he said, "so a few prosecutions and you could do away with a lot—in fact most pornography on the Internet."[85]

In order for obscenity laws to be enforced, a prosecutor must prove that the material in question is, in fact, obscene. The Supreme Court has ruled that obscenity is a value judgment that changes with the times and therefore must be determined by contemporary community standards. And one community's view of obscenity might be entirely different from another community's view. For example, residents of New York City might see obscenity in a completely different light from residents of Lubbock, Texas. Since the Internet can be accessed from all communities, however, the "community" for determining what is obscene on the Internet would most likely be the United States in its entirety

"Given that we live in a sea of pornography, it's hard to prove that anything violates these [community] standards these days."[86]

— Amy Adler, a law professor at New York University.

(though the courts are still unclear about this point). It is the laxity of these community standards that prevents prosecution. "The problem is, given that we live in a sea of pornography, it's hard to prove that anything violates these [community] standards these days,"[86] explains Amy Adler, a law professor at New York University. All a defense attorney needs to do, she says, is point out that the public cannot consider hardcore online pornography to be a violation of their standards of decency when, according to most experts, 70 percent of men and 30 percent of women regularly access it. According to Adler, this is why the Obama administration shuttered the Obscenity Prosecution Task Force in 2011: Obscenity is simply too difficult to prove.

Law enforcement authorities display photos of people arrested along with equipment seized as part of a 2014 investigation into online child pornography. Authorities hope that investigations such this will help stop child porn.

## Online Child Pornography Carries Harsh Sentences

Even though the federal government no longer prosecutes obscenity online, it takes the prosecution of online child pornography very seriously. With the help of large Internet corporations like Google, the government monitors Internet searches, browser histories, and e-mails for evidence of child pornography.

The FBI has also posted fake links to child pornography sites in order to catch those who are attempting to access them. Even though there is still a great deal of child pornography online, the government has been effective in its efforts. For instance, in March 2014 one of the largest online child pornography rings was shut down by the US Department of Homeland Security. A website on the Tor network (an online network that allows users to remain anonymous) featured more than 250 child victims who had been enticed to perform on webcams in more than thirty-nine US states and five foreign countries. Fourteen people were charged with conspiracy to produce child pornography in the sting, which was dubbed Operation Round Table.

Prison sentences for online child pornography violations have also increased. Since 1996 federal sentences for possession or distribution have increased by 500 percent. Under federal law, downloading a single image of child pornography is punishable by a mandatory minimum sentence of five years. In 2013 the average child pornography sentence was ten years, which is about the same as the average sentence for a physical sex crime. In addition, since 2006 the Federal Bureau of Prisons has been allowed to keep inmates past their release date if it believes the inmates will have a compulsion to commit sex crimes upon release—a process known as "civil commitment." In other words, child pornography offenders can be kept in prison for many years longer than their sentence without an additional trial.

## Online Child Pornography Leading to Child Sexual Abuse

One reason that penalties are so harsh is that they are intended to deter people from using child pornography. Production of child porn has exploded since the advent of the Internet, and lawmakers hope that a sufficiently harsh deterrent will decrease demand. Another reason for harsh penalties is that many experts believe that people who look at child pornography are likely to abuse children in real life. Studies conducted at the Butner Federal Correctional Institution's sex offender treatment program have confirmed this, including a 2009 study that tracked 155 men who had been convicted of crimes involving child pornography. Over the course of their treatment, 85 percent admitted they had also abused children in real life. In total, the group admitted to abusing 1,777 victims, about 13 per convict.

However, it recently has come to light that the Butner studies—which have been used by lawmakers to support the need for harsher sentences for more than a decade—may be flawed. Several former Butner patients have testified that psychologists routinely dropped patients from the program and returned them to prison—an especially dangerous environment for child sex offenders—if they felt a patient was not being frank about his past offenses. One such former patient is Sean Francis, who claims that in order to stay in the "safe confines of Butner,"[87] he invented fifty-four victims. Francis testified in his civil commitment hearing that most Butner patients invented crimes to stay in the program and that patients would often give each other advice about how to make their criminal history seem more realistic. "We shared victim lists," he said. "So I would go and I would say, 'Jim, show me what you have. Oh, that—that's really good.'"[88]

## Many Online Child Pornography Users Are Not Dangerous

The most recent research indicates that a growing proportion of people who access online child pornography are not potential child molesters. Michael Seto, a professor of psychiatry at the University of Toronto, found that online child pornography offenders who had not sexually abused children had a very different psychological profile from those who had. Those who operated only online did not have any antisocial traits such as impulsiveness and lack of empathy—traits common to all types of criminals, including child molesters. Seto called these online-only offenders "fantasy offenders." He claims that people who only look at child pornography online are extending their sexual fantasies into an environment that encourages a lack of inhibition. According to Seto, these people "may do and say things they would never dare in real life."[89]

"We have prisons now filled with guys . . . [who] pushed the wrong buttons, went too far and got into child porn."[90]

— John Grisham, best-selling author.

The courtroom thriller writer John Grisham recently spoke out about the problem of unfair sentencing for online child pornography offenses. "We have prisons now filled with guys my age. Sixty-year-old white men in prison who've never harmed anybody, would never touch a child. But they got online one night and started surfing around, probably had too much to drink or whatever, and pushed the wrong buttons, went too far and got into child porn."[90] Grisham was accused of defending pedophiles, and he quickly apologized for his comments. However, many experts

## Unfair Sentencing

The increasingly harsh sentences for online child pornography crimes are the result of an attitude among law enforcement and lawmakers that viewing child pornography is equivalent to actual sex abuse. Many people believe that those who seek out child pornography online have or will sexually abuse a child. The result is what some people consider to be a discrepancy in sentencing; viewing child pornography is sometimes punished more harshly than physically molesting a child. For instance, federal public defender Troy Stabenow has shown that "a defendant with no prior criminal record and no history of abusing children would qualify for a sentence of 15 to 20 years based on a small collection of child pornography and one photo swap, while a 50-year-old man who encountered a 13-year-old girl online and lured her into a sexual relationship would get no more than four years."

Quoted in Jacob Sullum, "What John Grisham Got Right About Child Pornography," *Time*, October 21, 2014. http://time.com.

agree that at least some of the people convicted on charges of child pornography are not actually pedophiles and pose no danger to children. For instance, a study by the federal Child Pornography Offenses sentencing committee found that when 610 child pornography offenders were tracked for 8.5 years after their release, only 7 percent were arrested for a new sexual offense. "There does exist a distinct group of offenders who are Internet-only and do not present a significant risk for hands-on sex offending,"[91] says Karl Hanson, a senior research officer at Public Safety Canada. These individuals may very well be addicted to online pornography in general and are simply searching for the most shocking and taboo material they can find.

## New Laws Are Problematic

Lawmakers rarely oppose laws that fight online child pornography. However, new laws that attempt to regulate online pornography that depicts adults usually fail at the federal level. Because of this, states are taking action, passing laws that attempt to close loopholes and better protect their residents. However, they often run into the same issues with the First Amendment as federal lawmakers do. One example is legislation that tries to outlaw revenge porn—pornography that is posted online for the purpose of humiliating the person in the image or video. California enacted such a law in 2013, making revenge porn a form of disorderly conduct. However, the law was significantly watered down before it could be passed so that it would not impinge on First Amendment rights. For instance, the law states that prosecutors must prove that the image was distributed with the intention to cause harm, not simply to encourage important public discourse—such as discourse about the moral character of a politician running for office.

*Forbes* uses the example of Representative Anthony Weiner, who was caught sending pornographic pictures of himself to women over the Internet. Weiner's pornographic selfies ultimately ruined his political career. "Any law restricting a recipient's redistribution of those images may substantially hinder important social discourses," legal writer Eric Goldman explains. "Weiner's sexting photos provide crucial evidence of his dubious decision-making and recidivism, so any law that interfered with their disclosure may violate the First Amendment."[92] This was just one of many exceptions written into the California law. Because the final version was so limited in scope, many experts doubt it will make a difference in reducing revenge pornography.

## Internet Filters Block More than Pornography

In the United Kingdom the government has decided to fight online pornography by bypassing the process of law. Prime Minister David Cameron's administration convinced the UK's four major Internet service providers (ISPs) to impose parental control Internet filters on all of their customers, automatically blocking pornographic and

*Representative Anthony Weiner of New York was caught sending sexually suggestive pictures of himself to women over the Internet. His sexted selfies ruined his political career.*

other unsavory content. The purpose of this policy is to help parents protect young children from inappropriate material. To opt out of the filters to get access to pornographic sites, each user must contact their ISP and request that filtering be removed.

The practice has drawn criticism on a global scale. The Open Rights Group, a nonprofit dedicated to freedom on the Internet, has claimed that people are unlikely to opt out of filtering because they will in essence be admitting that they watch pornography. In addition, the filters block much more than pornography. Each ISP has multiple levels of filters that block everything from sites that mention alcohol and smoking to sites that feature esoteric material—an undefined category that could include virtually anything.

As the program gets underway, Internet users are complaining that whole sections of the Internet are now blocked, including suicide prevention sites and other nonprofits. Some are also accusing the government of using filters to deliberately restrict access to information it does not want the public to have. For instance, the *Guardian* notes:

> The category of "obscene content", for instance . . . covers "sites with information about illegal manipulation of electronic devices [and] distribution of software"—in other words, filesharing and music downloads, debate over which has been going on in parliament for years. It looks as if that debate has just been bypassed entirely. . . . Whatever your opinion on downloading music and cartoons for free, doing so is neither obscene nor pornographic.[93]

Because of this level of censorship, many are wondering if the government's program to protect children from online pornography was merely an excuse to control the public's access to all types of information. As the Open Rights Group asserts, if protecting children was the aim, the government could have taken the ISPs' suggestion to require all customers to choose filtering levels. Regardless of the intent, the current situation in the United Kingdom makes it clear that widespread use of Internet filters to block pornography can have unintended consequences on freedom.

## Accountability Software

While it is clear that widespread use of Internet filters can restrict information, many individuals find them to be an effective tool to restrict access to online pornography. Online filtering software like Net Nanny do a fairly good job of protecting young children in the home from inadvertently being exposed to pornography—

## The Children's Internet Protection Act

One law that restricts online pornography is the Children's Internet Protection Act (CIPA). CIPA requires that all public schools and libraries that receive federal funds use Internet filtering software that blocks child pornography and obscenity. It also must block any material that is considered harmful to minors, such as legal pornography, Libraries may lift Internet filtering for adults who they determine are doing legitimate research. Unfortunately, Internet filtering software often blocks non-pornographic material such as health and medical information. In addition, some libraries are unable to lift filters because of the nature of their filtering software, and most cannot customize the filters used on wireless Internet connections. The result is that some libraries inadvertently block access to a great deal of information that is not only legal for adults to access but that also poses no threat to minors. Many libraries have objected to CIPA for this reason.

though experts claim that older children can usually find a way to circumvent the filters. But Internet filters are not just for children. Another type of Internet filter, called accountability software, is designed to help individuals who feel that they are addicted to online pornography. Instead of filtering pornography, this type of software tracks the sites an individual visits. The accountability software company Covenant Eyes explains the concept on its website: "What if you could send a report of your Internet activity to a friend or mentor so you could talk about where you struggle online? . . . Internet Accountability is a report of your Internet activities. . . . For adults, it means the temptation to click on inappropriate and pornographic links is reduced." Covenant Eyes even offers a way to cut off all

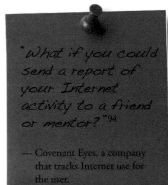

"What if you could send a report of your Internet activity to a friend or mentor?"[94]

— Covenant Eyes, a company that tracks Internet use for the user.

Internet access completely by clicking a "panic button" on its interface, designed for "when someone is struggling with temptation online."[94] Many people have found accountability software helps them break their addiction to online pornography by harnessing the power of peer pressure and the fear of embarrassment.

## Treatment Options

When individuals cannot break their addiction to online pornography on their own, various support groups and treatment programs are available. Sexaholics Anonymous and similar 12-step programs also address pornography addiction, and many sex addiction treatment programs have added online pornography addiction to the list of services they offer. In addition, many therapists now treat both sex addiction and pornography addiction on an outpatient basis.

Nearly all treatment programs for online pornography addiction call for complete abstinence. Addicts must give up both online pornography and masturbation—sometimes for life. Only healthy expressions of sexuality are permitted, such as sex within marriage or with a primary partner. According to sex addiction therapist Paula Hall, "For most [addicts], a period of celibacy and abstinence from masturbation can be useful to allow old neural pathways to begin to die."[95] Hall and other pornography addiction experts believe that if the old associations with sexual arousal are broken and replaced with healthier, more desirable patterns, then addiction can be overcome.

Abstinence is the principal behind the online self-help group NoFap, which challenges people to give up masturbating (or "fapping") to pornography. The group was started in response to a thread on the social media site Reddit that claimed that abstaining from ejaculating for seven days can significantly boost testosterone levels in men. While there is some scientific support for the idea, those who take the NoFap challenge report many other benefits. Some use it to self-treat their online pornography addiction, claiming that abstaining from masturbation restores their dopamine to normal levels and cures pornography-induced sexual dysfunction. Others say it gives them increased self-control and motivation,

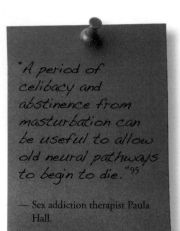

"A period of celibacy and abstinence from masturbation can be useful to allow old neural pathways to begin to die."[95]

— Sex addiction therapist Paula Hall.

improves their self-confidence, and even makes them more attractive to the opposite sex. The NoFap website states: "Many nofappers described increased happiness throughout their lives, especially in their attitudes towards sex and interpersonal relationships."[96] Currently, NoFap has more than one hundred thousand members.

## Online Pornography Benefits Society

Many people do not believe online pornography is a problem for society. Some object to the theory of pornography addiction and claim that overuse of online pornography is simply a symptom of an underlying emotional or interpersonal issue. Others object to the claim that pornography portrays women as victims. The organization We Consent, a networking and support group for women who work in or study the sex industry, believes that the moral panic over online pornography confuses extreme sex with lack of consent. We Consent claims that anti-pornography activists are

*Many types of Internet filtering software exist to help parents keep young children from accidentally being exposed to inappropriate Web content. These programs may be less useful for older children, who often find ways to get around the filters.*

anti-feminist: "They effectively say that regardless of how much autonomy, education, and will of personality a woman has, she cannot consent to being in [extreme] porn."[97]

We Consent claims that online pornography is actually a positive force in society. The group's website claims that porn saves relationships because it "fills the gap between a couple's differences in libidos"; it encourages new technology; it teaches about the body and expands notions about what sex can be; and the pornography industry empowers female stars by allowing them to set boundaries and limits. It claims that it is the anti-pornography activists who "fundamentally see women as victims, which in turn encourages women to see themselves as victims."[98]

In a discussion hosted by the debate organization Intelligence Squared titled "Pornography Is Good for Us: Without It We Would Be a Far More Repressed Society," academic researcher Clarissa Smith claimed that anti-pornography research tends to portray online pornography consumers as addicted deviants. They assume consumers are "incompetent and damaged" instead of asking them why they enjoy watching pornography. Smith and her colleagues are trying to answer that question by surveying more than five thousand individuals who enjoy online pornography. Initial results show that "porn is an important leisure activity for many people,"[99] says Smith.

Smith also objects to the notion that violent, explicit gonzo porn is what most people watch. She claims that the Internet has made it possible for there to be a type of pornography to fit every sensibility. According to Smith, online pornography "is representative of widely changing attitudes about sex, relationships, identity, the body, and the place of technologies in intimate life."[100]

Finally, some people believe the debate about whether pornography helps or harms society misses the point. Noted feminist Germaine Greer, who supports nonviolent and nonexploitive porn, claimed in the Intelligence Squared debate, "Pornography doesn't make us less repressed. Pornography is a way of making money out of the fact that we are repressed." Greer objects to the proliferation of online pornography because it makes sex ordinary.

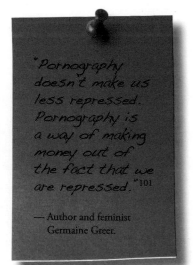

"Pornography doesn't make us less repressed. Pornography is a way of making money out of the fact that we are repressed."[101]

— Author and feminist Germaine Greer.

She says that online pornography is to sex what fast food is to eating, creating people who are "always full, but never satisfied." According to Greer, "Pornography replaces the possibility of real encounters with real people with stereotypical fantasy. . . . Pornography is like housework, only to be done again and again, repetitive, meaningless."[101] Greer believes that the real harm that online pornography poses is that it limits the human experience.

## Sex Will Always Be Controversial

The debate over the dangers and merits of online pornography to relationships parallels similar controversies about sex and violence in the media. Rock and roll was criticized for its sexual content, heavy metal music was said to contribute to teen suicide, graphic video games have been blamed for school shootings, and the sex and violence in the mainstream media has been blamed for a host of societal ills. Despite this current controversy there is no indication that online pornography will lose popularity in the United States anytime soon.

**Facts**

- According to Gary Wilson, an important step in recovering from pornography addiction is to stop using pornography to deal with stress, anxiety, and emotional pain.

- The addiction treatment center The Ranch claims that, like alcoholics, pornography addicts must abstain from using pornography for life.

- Jonathan Doyle, founder of StopUsingPornography.com, claims forming a supportive network or joining a support groups is a key component to successful recovery from pornography addiction.

- Four 12-step programs in the United States deal with sex and pornography addiction: Sex Addicts Anonymous, Sexaholics Anonymous, Sex and Love Addicts Anonymous, and Sexual Compulsives Anonymous.

# Source Notes

## Introduction: The Internet Is for Porn

1. Quoted in Julie Ruvolo, "The Internet Is for Porn (So Let's Talk About It)," *Forbes,* May 20, 2011. www.forbes.com.
2. Sebastian Anthony, "Just How Big Are Porn Sites?," *ExtremeTech* (blog), April 4, 2012. www.extremetech.com.
3. Quoted in Mark Ward, "Web Porn: Just How Much Is There?," BBC News, June 30, 2013. www.bbc.com.

## Chapter One: What Are the Origins of the Online Pornography Controversy?

4. Ronald Ostrow, "Fight Against Child Pornography Waged on New Front: Computers," *Los Angeles Times,* September 1, 1993. http://articles.latimes.com.
5. Quoted in Scott Powers, "Controversy Continues over *Time*'s Story on 'Cyberporn' and the Internet," *Baltimore (MD) Sun,* July 23, 1995. http://articles.baltimoresun.com.
6. Quoted in Powers, "Controversy Continues over *Time*'s Story on 'Cyberporn' and the Internet."
7. Peter Schorsch, "TBT: Supreme Court Rulings on Cyberporn, Sodomy, and DOMA," *SaintPetersBlog,* June 26, 2014. www.saintpetersblog.com.
8. Quoted in CNN, "Internet Indecency Case Gets Under Way," March 21, 1996. www.cnn.com.
9. Quoted in CNN, "Internet Indecency Case Gets Under Way."
10. John Paul Stevens, Reno v. American Civil Liberties Union, 521 US 844, 1997, US Supreme Court Syllabus, in Find Law for Legal Professionals, June 26, 1997. www.caselaw.lp.findlaw.com.
11. Quoted in Linda Greenhouse, "'Virtual' Child Pornography Ban Overturned," *New York Times*, April 17, 2002. www.nytimes.com.
12. Michael Stabile, "End of the Porn Golden Age," *Salon*, March 2, 2012. www.salon.com.
13. Paul Rudo, "Ten Indispensable Technologies Built by the Pornography Industry," Enterprise Features, June 5, 2011. www.enterprisefeatures.com.
14. Quoted in Oxymoron Entertainment, "Interview with Christopher Mallick from Oxymoron Entertainment," Vimeo, June 29, 2012. http://vimeo.com.
15. Quoted in Ross Benes, "Porn: The Hidden Engine That Drives Innovation in Tech," Business Insider, July 5, 2013. www.businessinsider.com.
16. Quoted in Stabile, "End of the Porn Golden Age."

17. Quoted in Matthew Little, "Pornography Ruins Healthy Relationships, Says Expert," *Epoch Times,* November 21, 2013. http://theepochtimes .com.

## Chapter Two: How Addictive Is Online Pornography?

18. Quoted in Napp Naxworth, "Internet Porn Pandemic Threatens World and Church, Apologetics Conference Highlights," *Christian Post*, October 17, 2014. www.christianpost.com.
19. Stanton Peele, "Addiction in Society: Blinded by Biochemistry," *Psychology Today*, June 15, 2011. www.psychologytoday.com.
20. American Society of Addiction Medicine, "Definition of Addiction," April 19, 2011. www.asam.org.
21. National Institute on Drug Abuse, "The Science of Drug Abuse and Addiction: The Basics," *Media Guide*, September 2014. www.drugabuse.gov.
22. Elizabeth Hartney, "What Are Behavioral Addictions?," About Health, April 9, 2014. http://addictions.about.com.
23. Candéo, "Pornography Is a Drug," 2014. http://candeobehaviorchange .com.
24. Gary Wilson, *The Great Porn Experiment*, TEDxGlasgow, YouTube, May 16, 2012. www.youtube.com.
25. Gary Wilson, "Without the Coolidge Effect There Would Be No Internet Porn," Your Brain on Porn, August 8, 2011. www.yourbrainonporn.com.
26. Quoted in Fight the New Drug, "Porn Is like a Drug," August 8, 2014. http://fightthenewdrug.org.
27. Quoted in Jillian Keenan, "Is Sex Addiction Real or Just an Excuse?," *Slate,* July 24, 2013. www.slate.com.
28. Quoted in Julie Bindel, "Without Porn, the World Would Be a Better Place," *Guardian* (London), October 24, 2014. www.theguardian.com.
29. Quoted in Bindel, "Without Porn, the World Would Be a Better Place."
30. Fight the New Drug, "Porn Affects Your Behavior," August 8, 2014. http://fightthenewdrug.org.
31. Quoted in Heather Bohlender, "Porn," *Onward* (blog), March 16, 2012. http://heatherbo.blogspot.com.
32. Quoted in Norma Costello, "Porn-Aholic: A Love of Porn Transformed into a Serious Addiction," *Independent.ie* (Dublin, Ireland), July 13, 2014. www.independent.ie.
33. Quoted in Costello, "Porn-Aholic."
34. Andrea Poe, "5 Things Your Employees Are Doing Right Now Instead of Working," AllBusiness.com. www.allbusiness.com.
35. Quoted in Julie Bindel, "The Truth About the Porn Industry," *Guardian* (London), July 2, 2010. www.theguardian.com.
36. Marty Klein, "You're Addicted to What?," *Humanist*, June 28, 2012. http://thehumanist.com.
37. Quoted in Tracy Clark-Flory, "Porn, Addictive? There's No Proof," *Salon,* February 15, 2014. www.salon.com.
38. Quoted in Clark-Flory, "Porn, Addictive? There's No Proof."
39. Quoted in Clark-Flory, "Porn, Addictive? There's No Proof."

40. Quoted in Reboot Blueprint, "How to Overcome a Porn Addiction: Advice from 10 Influential Sex Health Writers." http://rebootblueprint.com.

41. Asiafilm, comment on Amy O'Leary, "So How Do We Talk About This? When Children See Online Pornography," *New York Times*, May 9, 2012. www.nytimes.com.

42. Michael Robinson, comment on O'Leary, "So How Do We Talk About This?"

43. Paul, comment on O'Leary, "So How Do We Talk About This?"

44. Boo, comment on O'Leary, "So How Do We Talk About This?"

45. Linsey Davis and Jackie Pou, via *Nightline*, "Sex Obsessed: Is the Average Teen Brain Ready for Porn?," ABC News, October 31, 2013.

46. Gail Dines, interview by Martin Daubney, *Porn on the Brain,* Channel 4 (UK television network), September 30, 2013. http://thoughtmaybe.com.

47. Quoted in Martin Daubney, "Experiment That Convinced Me Online Porn Is the Most Pernicious Threat Facing Children Today," MailOnline, September 25, 2013. www.dailymail.co.uk.

48. Daubney, "Experiment That Convinced Me Online Porn Is the Most Pernicious Threat Facing Children Today."

49. Linsey Davis and Jackie Pou, via *Nightline*, "Sex Obsessed: Is the Average Teen Brain Ready for Porn?," ABC News, October 31, 2013.

50. Quoted in David Segal, "Does Porn Hurt Children?," *New York Times,* March 28, 2014. www.nytimes.com.

51. Respect Yourself, "Porn Facts," 2014. www.respectyourself.info.

52. Quoted in Segal, "Does Porn Hurt Children?"

53. Daubney, "Experiment That Convinced Me Online Porn Is the Most Pernicious Threat Facing Children Today."

54. Quoted in Morgan Lee, "Former Porn Magazine Editor Now Warns Parents to Protect Children from It," *Christian Post*, October 1, 2013. www.christianpost.com.

55. Robert Weiss, "Is Male Porn Use Ruining Sex?," *Love and Sex in the Digital Age* (blog), *Psychology Today*, January 20, 2014. www.psychologytoday.com.

56. Weiss, "Is Male Porn Use Ruining Sex?"

57. Gary Wilson, interview by Max J. Van Pragg, "About High-Speed Internet Porn Addiction, with Gary Wilson," *PrivateMattersTVShow*, December 12, 2012. www.youtube.com.

58. Isaac Abel, "Did Porn Warp Me Forever?," *Salon*, January 12, 2013. www.salon.com.

59. Daubney, "Experiment That Convinced Me Online Porn Is the Most Pernicious Threat Facing Children Today."

60. Quoted in Associated Press, "Anchorage Youths Face Child Porn Charges," in *Washington Times*, May 13, 2014. www.washingtontimes.com.

61. Quoted in Ken Edelstein, "Teens Face More Consequences from Sexting than Congressmen Do," Reclaiming Futures, June 14, 2011. http://reclaimingfutures.org.

62. Quoted in Segal, "Does Porn Hurt Children?"

63. Quoted in Clark-Flory, "Porn, Addictive? There's No Proof."

64. Quoted in Segal, "Does Porn Hurt Children?"

65. Linsey Davis and Jackie Pou, via *Nightline*, "Sex Obsessed: Is the Average Teen Brain Ready for Porn?," ABC News, October 31, 2013.

## Chapter Four: How Does Online Pornography Affect Relationships?

66. Kevin Skinner, "How Porn Really Affects Relationships," *Inside Porn Addiction* (blog), *Psychology Today*, August 5, 2014. www.psychologytoday.com.

67. Tony Lister, "Porn Cure: Addiction Straight Talk—Shame Cycle," curethecraving.com, YouTube, April 30, 2011. www.youtube.com.

68. Lister, "Porn Cure."

69. Fight the New Drug, "Porn Affects Your Behavior."

70. Vicki Larson, "Does Porn Watching Lead to Divorce?," *Huffington Post*, May 29, 2011. www.huffingtonpost.com.

71. Maria, "Maria's Story: How Porn Affected Her Marriage," Fight the New Drug, August 4, 2014. http://fightthenewdrug.org.

72. Wilson, *The Great Porn Experiment*.

73. Quoted in Taryn Hillin, "Study Says Your Spouse's Porn Habit Might Not Be So Harmless After All," *Huffington Post*, May 9, 2014. www.huffingtonpost.com.

74. Wilson, *The Great Porn Experiment*.

75. Quoted in Clark-Flory, "Porn, Addictive? There's No Proof."

76. Quoted in Clark-Flory, "Porn, Addictive? There's No Proof."

77. Quoted in Clark-Flory, "Porn, Addictive? There's No Proof."

78. Nichi Hodgson, "The Intimate Confessions of a Female Porn Fan," *Telegraph* (UK), August 7, 2014. www.telegraph.co.uk.

79. Quoted in Stacey Nelkin, "5 Reasons Why Watching Porn Together Can Be Good for Your Relationship," *Huffington Post*, March 7, 2013. www.huffingtonpost.com.

80. Hodgson, "The Intimate Confessions of a Female Porn Fan."

81. Quoted in Larson, "Does Porn Watching Lead to Divorce?"

82. Quoted in Larson, "Does Porn Watching Lead to Divorce?"

83. Quoted in Larson, "Does Porn Watching Lead to Divorce?"

84. Marty Klein, "Porn Addict or Selfish Bastard? Life Is More Complicated than That," *Sexual Intelligence* (blog), *Psychology Today*, May 6, 2011. www.psychologytoday.com.

## Chapter Five: What Should Be Done About Online Pornography?

85. Quoted in Thomas Cloud, "Obama Administration Urged to Enforce Laws Against Hard-Core Pornography," CNS News, April 9, 2012. http://cnsnews.com.

86. Quoted in E. Alex Jung, "Who Gives a S---?," Al Jazeera, February 17, 2014. http://america.aljazeera.com.

87. Quoted in Rachel Aviv, "The Science of Sex Abuse," *New Yorker*, January 14, 2013. www.newyorker.com.

88. Quoted in Aviv, "The Science of Sex Abuse."

89. Quoted in Aviv, "The Science of Sex Abuse."

90. Quoted in Jessica Goldstein, "Everything Wrong with John Grisham's Defense of Old Guys Who Look at Child Pornography," *ThinkProgress* (blog), October 16, 2014. http://thinkprogress.org.

91. Jacob Sullum, "What John Grisham Got Right About Child Pornography," *Time,* October 21, 2014. http://time.com.

92. Eric Goldman, "California's New Law Shows It's Not Easy to Regulate Revenge Porn," *Forbes*, October 8, 2013. www.forbes.com.

93. Laurie Penny, "David Cameron's Internet Porn Filter Is the Start of Censorship Creep," *Guardian* (London), January 3, 2014. www.theguardian .com.

94. Covenant Eyes, "Internet Accountability," 2014. www.covenanteyes.com.

95. Paula Hall, *Understanding and Treating Sex Addiction*. New York: Routledge, 2013. Kindle edition.

96. "What Is NoFap?," NoFap. www.nofap.org.

97. We Consent, "Pornography," 2012. www.weconsent.org.

98. We Consent, "Pornography."

99. Quoted in Intelligence Squared, *Pornography Is Good for Us: Without It We Would Be a Far More Repressed Society*, video, April 23, 2013. www.intel ligencesquared.com.

100. Quoted in Intelligence Squared, *Pornography Is Good for Us*.

101. Quoted in Intelligence Squared, *Pornography Is Good for Us*.

# Related Organizations and Websites

## Enough Is Enough (EIE)

746 Walker Rd., Suite 116
Great Falls, VA 22066
phone: (703) 476-7890
fax: (703) 476-7894
website: www.protectkids.com

The EIE is a nonprofit organization dedicated to protecting children in cyberspace. Its online resource Protect Kids contains numerous articles about teens and online pornography.

## Fight the New Drug

phone: (385) 313-8629
website: www.fightthenewdrug.org

Fight the New Drug's mission is to raise awareness on the harmful effects of pornography. Its website contains information and resources aimed at helping teenagers and adults deal with the effects of pornography use.

## Free Speech Coalition

370 Maple Ave. W., Suite 4
Vienna, Virginia 22180-5615
phone: (703) 356-6912
fax: (703) 356-5085
website: www.freespeechcoalition.org

The Free Speech Coalition is a nonprofit trade association of the adult entertainment industry dedicated to protecting First Amendment rights through activism and lobbying. Its blog contains news about the pornography industry and the law.

## Kinsey Institute

Morrison Hall 302
1165 E. Third St.
Bloomington, IN 47405
phone: (812) 855-7686
fax: (812) 855-8277
e-mail: kinsey@indiana.edu
website: www.kinseyinstitute.org

The Kinsey Institute conducts research to advance sexual health and knowledge about critical issues in sex, gender, and reproduction. The institute is an excellent source of facts and statistics about sexual issues and behavior, including pornography use.

## Morality in Media

1100 G St. NW #1030
Washington, DC 20005
phone: (202) 393-7245
website: moralityinmedia.org
website: http://pornharms.com

Morality in Media is a national nonprofit organization dedicated to opposing online obscenity and indecency through public education and application of the law. Its companion website, Porn Harms, contains news and resources specific to online pornography.

## NoFap

website: www.nofap.org

NoFap is an online community-based organization that hosts challenges in which participants abstain from pornography use or masturbation for a period of time. NoFap has a community of more than one hundred thousand members who share information about problems associated with online pornography.

## Sex Addicts Anonymous (SAA)

PO Box 70949
Houston, TX 77270
phone: (800) 477-8191
e-mail: info@ssa-recovery.com
website: https://saa-recovery.org

The SAA is one of the few 12-step sex and pornography addiction programs that specifically welcomes women and has a large female membership. SAA uses the book *Sex Addicts Anonymous*, also known as *The*

*Green Book*. It is available on its website along with the SAA newsletter and other educational information.

## Sexaholics Anonymous (SA)

PO Box 3565
Brentwood, TN 37024
phone: (615) 370-6062  •  toll-free: (866) 424-8777
fax: (615) 370-0882
e-mail: saico@sa.org
website: www.sa.org

The SA is the only 12-step program that defines sexual sobriety for its members as no masturbation or sex outside of marriage. The SA uses the book *Sexaholics Anonymous*, also known as *The White Book*, which is available on its website along with other educational information.

## Sex and Love Addicts Anonymous (SLAA)

1550 NE Loop 410, Suite 118
San Antonio, TX 78209
phone: (210) 439-1123
e-mail: info@slaafws.org
website: www.slaafws.org

Created by members of Alcoholics Anonymous in 1976, the SLAA was the first 12-step program to address sex and pornography addictions. It is also one of the largest, with more than 16,000 members and 1,200 meetings in 43 countries. The SLAA uses the book *Sex and Love Addicts Anonymous*, also known as *S.L.A.A. Basic Text*. Its website contains resources and an online store.

## Sexual Compulsives Anonymous (SCA)

PO Box 1585
Old Chelsea Station
New York, NY 10011
phone: (800) 977-4325
website: www.sca-recovery.org

The SCA was originally formed to address issues of sexual compulsion among gay and bisexual men. It developed its own sex and pornography compulsion screening test called "The Twenty Questions," which is available on its website along with its primary book, *Sexual Compulsives Anonymous*, and other educational material.

### Sexual Recovery Institute (SRI)

1964 Westwood Boulevard, Suite 400
Los Angeles, CA 90025
phone: (844) 299-8162
fax: (424) 832-3214
website: www.sexualrecovery.com

The SRI is one of the world's top sex addiction treatment centers. It was founded in 1995 by Robert Weiss, who based its intensive two-week recovery program on the theories of sex addiction developed by Patrick J. Carnes. The SRI's website contains a wealth of educational material about sex and pornography addiction.

## Your Brain on Porn

website: www.yourbrainonporn.com

Your Brain on Porn was founded by science writer Gary Wilson. The website contains a wealth of information on pornography addiction, addiction recovery, and links to news about online pornography in the media.

# Additional Reading

## Books

Marty Klein, *America's War on Sex.* Santa Barbara, CA: Praeger, 2012.

David Ley, *The Myth of Sex Addiction.* Lanham, MD: Rowman & Littlefield, 2012.

Ogi Ogas and Sai Gaddam, *A Billion Wicked Thoughts: What the World's Largest Experiment Reveals About Human Desire.* New York: Dutton, 2011.

Susanna Paasonen, *Carnal Resonance: Affect and Online Pornography.* Boston: MIT, 2011.

Robert Weiss and Jennifer P. Schneider, *Closer Together, Further Apart: The Effect of Technology and the Internet on Parenting, Work, and Relationships.* Carefree, AZ: Gentle Path, 2014. E-book.

## Periodicals

Rachel Aviv, "The Science of Sex Abuse," *New Yorker*, January 14, 2013.

Julie Bindel, "Without Porn, the World Would Be a Better Place," *Guardian* (London), October 24, 2014.

Nichi Hodgson, "The Intimate Confessions of a Female Porn Fan," *Telegraph* (London), August 7, 2014.

Julie Ruvolo, "The Internet Is for Porn (So Let's Talk About It)," *Forbes,* May 20, 2011.

David Segal, "Does Porn Hurt Children?," *New York Times*, March 28, 2014.

Robert Weiss, "Is Male Porn Use Ruining Sex?," *Psychology Today*, January 20, 2014.

## Online Videos

Intelligence Squared, *Pornography Is Good for Us: Without It We Would Be a Far More Repressed Society*, April 23, 2013. www .intelligencesquared.com/events/pornography-is-good-for-us.

Gary Wilson, *The Great Porn Experiment*, TEDxGlasgow, YouTube, May 16, 2012. www.youtube.com/watch?v=wSF82AwSDiU.

## Internet Sources

Isaac Abel, "Did Porn Warp Me Forever?," *Salon*, January 12, 2013. www.salon.com/2013/01/13/did_porn_warp_me_forever.

Martin Daubney, "Experiment That Convinced Me Online Porn Is the Most Pernicious Threat Facing Children Today," MailOnline, September 25, 2013. www.dailymail.co.uk/fema il/article-2432591/Porn-pernicious-threat-facing-children-to day-By-ex-lads-mag-editor-MARTIN-DAUBNEY.html.

# Index